T0128380

ANTI-CALVINISM

GERALD W. MCDANIEL

WESTBOW
P R E S S®
A DIVISION OF THOMAS NELSON
& ZONDERVAN

WestBow Press books may be ordered through
booksellers or by contacting:

WestBow Press
A Division of Thomas Nelson & Zondervan
1663 Liberty Drive
Bloomington, IN 47403
www.westbowpress.com
1 (866) 928-1240

Scripture taken from the King James Version of the Bible.

ISBN: 978-1-9736-7872-4 (sc)
ISBN: 978-1-9736-7871-7 (e)

Print information available on the last page.

WestBow Press rev. date: 10/28/2019

Contents

A Personal Letter to my Grandchildren

I would like to share first of all a partial personal testimony out of my own life. Many years ago, as a small young boy I was extremely shy and very much an introvert. I would do most anything to avoid standing up in front of people and speaking especially in front of a school class. Even in sports on the basketball court the intimidation of the crowd no matter how large or small would greatly hinder me from playing basketball as well as I was able.

I had a dear grandmother who was a precious Christian lady. When she would come to stay with our family from time to time, she would always call me her little preacher boy. I hated it because even though I was lost at the time I knew that it would mean getting up in front of people. Needless to say, I regretted it every time grandmother came around.

At the age of 20 years old I trusted Christ as my personal Savior. At the age of 21 years old, strange as it may seem, God called me to preach. My grandmother was right.

Having said this, I am convinced just like grandmother was that I will have a grandchild whether born or adopted, girl or boy that God will call to take the books that I have written and learn them and be able to understand them and teach from them and use them in their ministry that God has for them.

Be advised. You will run into many that do not agree with the teachings in these books. You will probably have family that will not agree with the teachings in these books. Either way as a little girl in writing or teaching ladies or as a little boy in writing or teaching and preaching I am convinced God will raise up one of my grandchildren to a ministry that these books will be greatly used.

Please understand at the time of this writing there have been 4 books published and 2 written yet to be published with more to come. At this time, you may not even be born yet or adopted yet. Even though all my grandchildren are welcome to these books and will have access to these books and I am convinced as much as I am alive that God will raise up one of you with a special ministry directly related to these books.

If I live long enough, I will be able to witness this taking place first hand. My grandmother died before she was able to hear me preach. Please be aware that I am not writing these books as a hobby neither are they written to make money. It is a God called ministry. There will be many more books written and all my grandchildren will have access to them if that is their desire. I want to reassure you of course that I love all my grandchildren.

There will be one with a special calling. May God bless you little one and I am praying for you now even if you have not been born or adopted yet. Granddaddy loves you very much and is excited about what God will do in your life.

This writing will be published with the future books to make sure you get a copy of this letter.

Chapter 1

<u>The Plan of Salvation</u>

Let's go through **4 H's. Honesty, Humility, Helpless, and Hope**

H #1) *You must be **HONEST** enough to admit you have sinned and broken God's commands. Understand in doing so this puts you in very great danger!*
Romans 3:10 "there is none righteous, no not one."

Romans 3:23 "…all have sinned…"

I John 1:8 "if we say that we have no sin, we deceive ourselves, and the truth is not in us."

H #2) *You must be **HUMBLE** enough to admit you deserve Hell when you die. One sin disqualifies us from Heaven, and we have all sinned more than once.*
Romans 6:23 "For the wages of sin [is] death"

Revelation 21:8 "But the fearful, and unbelieving, and the abominable, and murderers, and whoremongers, and sorcerers, and idolaters, and all liars, shall have their part in the lake which burneth with fire and brimstone: which is the second death."

H #3) *You must understand you are **HELPLESS** when it comes to you saving yourself from going to Hell when you die. There is nothing you can do to pay for your own sin.*

Ephesians 2:8-9 For by grace are ye saved through faith; and that not of yourselves: it is the gift of God: not of works, lest any man should boast.

Titus 3:5 Not by works of righteousness which we have done, but according to his mercy he saved us, by the washing of regeneration, and renewing of the Holy Ghost;

Galatians 2:16 Knowing that a man is not justified by the works of the law, but by the faith of Jesus Christ, even we have believed in Jesus Christ, that we might be justified by the faith of Christ, and not by the works of the law: for by the works of the law shall no flesh be justified.

Understand when I say HELPLESS it means you cannot surrender your life to Christ for salvation. You have no life to surrender. You are dead in trespasses and sins. You cannot yet make Jesus the Lord of your life because you have no life. Jesus will not be Lord of your life until He is Savior of your soul. You cannot turn from your sins because you are dead in your sins. You must see yourself HELPLESS at the Mercy of God. Now you are ready for H # 4.

H #4) *You are helpless but not hopeless. Your **HOPE** must be in Jesus, God's Son and what he has done for you on the cross when He died there. Jesus is the only one that paid for your sins when he died on the cross. He was buried and arose again. You must ask Jesus to be your personal Savior and ask Jesus to save you from Hell. If you are depending on church membership to save you, that means you are not depending on Jesus to save you. If you are depending on the good deeds you do to save you, that means you are not depending on Jesus to save you. If you are depending on baptism to save you, that means you are not depending on Jesus to save you. It must be Jesus and what Jesus did for you on the cross that you are depending on to save you. Nothing else can go with this. Jesus is the only one who paid for your sins on the cross so Jesus is the only one who can save you.*

Romans 5:8 But God commendeth his love toward us, in that, while we were yet sinners, Christ died for us.

I Peter 3:18 For Christ also hath once suffered for sins, the just for the unjust, that he might bring us to God, being put to death in the flesh but quickened by the Spirit.

Hebrews 10:12 But this man (JESUS) after he hath offered one sacrifice for sins for ever, sat down on the right hand of God.

John 14:6 Jesus saith unto him, I am the way, the truth, and the life: no man cometh unto the Father, but by me.

Acts 4:12 Neither is there salvation in any other: for there is none other name under heaven given among men, whereby we must be saved.

John 3:16 For God so loved the world, that he gave his only begotten Son, that whosoever believeth in him should not perish, but have everlasting life.

Ask Jesus to save you before it is too late:
Romans 10:13 For whosoever shall call upon the name of the Lord shall be saved.

Chapter 2

<u>Opening Comments</u>

Calvinism is a system of false teachings from the 1500's in history. Many religions and denominations of all kinds have been entangled to some degree into some form of Calvinism. At one time in history for many years people of most any kind of religion were thought to be put into one of two different groups. The one group was called "Calvinism" and the other group was called "Armenianism." Sad to say neither system of teachings is totally correct.

The Calvinist label came from the individual Jon Calvin of 1509 to 1564 for his system of false teachings. However, some of these false teachings can be found in writings earlier in history before Jon Calvin.

The Armenian label came from the individual Jacobus Arminius of 1560 to 1609 for his system of false teachings. Again, some of these false teachings in this system can also be found in writings earlier in history before Jacobus Arminius.

All along through history there was always independent groups of believers and churches that taught the Bible and believed neither in Calvinism nor in Armenianism. These independent believers were labeled across the board as Anabaptists. Even though there were many types of independent churches and beliefs, all of them including the true Bible believers were labeled Anabaptists by their opposing religions. This label was given by those that opposed them and was meant as slander and was coming mainly from their Catholic neighbors.

The Calvinist believed in a distorted view of eternal security and a distorted view of predestination. The Armenian believed you could lose your salvation and believed in working to stay saved or that you must have works with faith to be saved but rejected the view of the Calvinist on predestination.

Many of those that were labeled Anabaptist rejected both the Calvinism and the Armenian teachings. They believed in eternal security but not in the view of the version of Predestination that the Calvinists taught. They knew that it was impossible to lose your salvation. So, they rejecting the teachings of the Armenian. Notice the following passages.

Acts 14:15 And saying, Sirs, why do ye these things? We also are men of like passions with you, and preach unto you that ye should turn from these vanities unto the living God, which made heaven, and earth, and the sea, and all things that are therein: **14:16** Who in times past suffered all nations to walk in their own ways. **14:17** Nevertheless **he left not himself without witness**, in that he did good, and gave us rain from heaven, and fruitful seasons, filling our hearts with food and gladness.

1John 5:9 If we receive the witness of men, **the witness of God is greater**: for this is the witness of God which he hath testified of his Son.

This author is neither Calvinists nor Armenian. Please see this author's book on "Eternal Security." This author does not believe it is possible to lose your salvation and does not believe everyone is unconditionally predestined to Heaven or Hell.

There are and were many well-known and big-named preachers and public speakers down through history who encouraged Calvinism and spread this false religion into many fundamental circles and churches and even have crossed over several denominational barriers. Not seeing the harm that it caused, many gullible believers were not aware that this deadly false teaching was coming in on the back of the Trojan horse of big named, famous, and popular preachers.

One of the things that make this teaching so deadly is that like any other false teaching, it cannot be backed up with the Scriptures. There are many bad side effects of Calvinism. To name a few, typically the person that believes like the Calvinist, loses their burden for spreading the Gospel, that is, if they have believed the gospel. They are taught that it is set in stone and already determined by God that everyone is predestined for Heaven or Hell. Another bad side effect of Calvinism is that it gives a horrible and false image of God Himself. When someone tells you that people are predestined for Hell and that there is nothing that they can do about it and there is no way out of Hell, it makes you wonder what kind of individual they think God is?

In this book you will be able to see and read about many passages in the Bible on this subject teaching against Calvinism. Along with this, you will see by explanation the passages in the Bible used out of context by the Calvinist to attempt to defend their beliefs but the passages are put in their proper context to expose the false teachings and errors of Calvinism.

Even the secular world has a tendency to think "whatever will be will be." Some assume every detail of our lives has already been predetermined which totally does away with the human free will of man. Man is not a robot or a machine. Man is given by his Creator the power and will to choose and man will face the consequences of each choice and answer to God for what he chooses. The greatest choice that man must face is to choose or reject Christ as Savior. The consequences of this choice are either eternity in Heaven or eternity in Hell. No one that goes to Hell can say it is God's fault that they are there. Hell was not even originally designed for humans. Notice the following passage.

Matthew 25:41 Then shall he say also unto them on the left hand, Depart from me, ye cursed, into everlasting fire, **prepared for the devil and his angels**:

It is because of man's own unbelief that man is condemned to Hell. See the following passages:

John 3:18 He that believeth on him is not condemned: but **he that believeth not is condemned already**, because **he hath not believed in the name of the only begotten Son of God**.

John 3:36 He that believeth on the Son hath everlasting life: and **he that believeth not the Son shall not see life; but the wrath of God abideth on him.**

As you go through this book you will find according to the Scriptures that God loves the entire human race and that means every individual on the planet. It is not God's will for anyone to go to Hell. Jesus died on the cross to pay for everyone's sin. Jesus died to pay for the sins of Adam and Eve and forward to all. Mankind is faced with the choice of choosing or rejecting Jesus Christ as their Savior. The will of man has a huge roll and factor in where man spends his eternity. The will of mankind must be aligned with the will of God for man to have any spiritual success in this life or in eternity.

Chapter 3

<u>T. U. L. I. P.</u>

In this chapter you will be getting the outline used by most Calvinist given to express their teachings and beliefs on Calvinism. Sometimes they are referred to as five-point Calvinist due to the five points of this outline that they use. You will see a concise explanation given on each point of the outline. In later chapters there will be given more details to each point of the outline and further explanation of why each point in the outline is not scriptural. If you are to believe and hold to the scriptures and believe what the Bible says you will neither be a five, four, three, two, or even one-point Calvinist and neither will you be an Armenian.

T—Total Depravity of Man (Please see **Chapter 4** for more detail.)

The Bible teaches that man has no ability to pay for his own sin and he must look to Jesus for salvation because He died on the cross for him and paid for his sins and he must trust in Jesus and what He did for him on the cross to save him from Hell.

The Calvinists say that man is so depraved that man has no ability to do anything for salvation and not even to believe. They say that man has no part in his own salvation. They teach that it is entirely up to God and that man has no say so in the matter at all and they teach that salvation is totally automatic.

U—Unconditional Election (Please see **Chapter 5** for more detail.)

The Calvinist teaches that God does the total choosing and that it is totally unconditional on man's part. The Calvinist actually teaches that man has no choice in the matter of salvation.

Election is conditional. Man must choose God's way by believing the truth about Jesus and then to trust Jesus as their personal Savior.

L—Limited Atonement (Please see **Chapter 6** for more detail.)

The Calvinist says Jesus only died for those who are going to be saved and not for those who are lost and reject Christ as Savior.

The Bible says Jesus died for the entire human race whether they get saved or not and that there is no limited atonement.

I—Irresistible Grace (Please see **Chapter 7** for more detail.)

The Calvinist says when God calls a man to salvation; the man has no choice in the matter. They say that this work of grace is irresistible. Man is not able to resist the call of grace for salvation.

However, the Jews resisted God's call to be saved many times and so have countless gentiles.

P—Perseverance of Saints (Please see **Chapter 8** for more detail.)

The Calvinist says we are eternally saved because saved man will persevere.

The Bible says we are eternally saved by God's grace and because we are saved, God will hang on to us. Our salvation is eternally secure because God hangs on to us and not because we hang on to God.

Chapter 4

<u>Total Depravity of Man?</u>

The Bible teaches that man has no ability to pay for his own sin and he must look to Jesus for salvation.

The Calvinists say man has no ability to do anything for salvation. They teach that God literally does everything for them.

There are many verses in the Bible that tell us of man's depravity and that man has sinned and broken God's commandments. See the following to name a few:

1 John 1:8 If we say that we have no sin, we deceive ourselves, and the truth is not in us.

1 John 1:10 If we say that we have not sinned, we make him a liar, and his word is not in us.

Romans 3:10 As it is written, There is none righteous, no, not one:

Romans 3:23 For all have sinned, and come short of the glory of God;

Ecclesiastes 7:20 For *there is* not a just man upon earth, that doeth good, and sinneth not.

However nowhere in the Bible can you find it to be taught that man's will is not involved in his decision of trusting Christ as his personal Savior. If man does not want salvation man does not get salvation. Note the following passage.

Revelation 22:17 And the Spirit and the bride say, Come. And let him that heareth say, Come. And let him that is athirst come. And **whosoever will**, let him take the water of life freely.

Man's works have no part in his salvation but man's will does have part in his salvation. No man ever got saved that did not want to get saved. This is why you cannot trick or badger a person into getting saved. We must present the plan of salvation as simple and as clear as possible with thorough explanation but the lost sinner must want to be saved.

However, before they can be saved, they must first see themselves lost and helpless when it comes to paying the penalty and price for their own sin.

See the following passages that isolate and separate man's works from salvation:

Ephesians 2:8–9 For by grace are ye saved through faith; and that not of yourselves: *it is* the gift of God: **9** Not of works, lest any man should boast.

Titus 3:5–7 Not by works of righteousness which we have done, but according to his mercy he saved us, by the washing of regeneration, and renewing of the Holy Ghost; **6** Which he shed on us abundantly through Jesus Christ our Saviour; **7** That being justified by his grace, we should be made heirs according to the hope of eternal life.

Galatians 2:16 Knowing that a man is not justified by the works of the law, but by the faith of Jesus Christ, even we have believed in Jesus Christ, that we might be justified by the faith of Christ, and not by the works of the law: for by the works of the law shall no flesh be justified.

The Bible tells us that there are certain things that man must do in order to be saved. The Calvinist says there is nothing that man can do for himself in order to be saved. However, the Bible says the lost man must do the following. God will not do these things for man.

a. Hear the word of God

Romans 10:17 So then faith *cometh* by hearing, and hearing by the word of God.

b. Understand what the Bible says on how to be saved

Matthew 13:15 For this people's heart is waxed gross, and *their* ears are dull of hearing, and their eyes they have closed;

lest at any time they should <u>see with their eyes</u>, and <u>hear with *their* ears,</u> and **should understand with *their* heart**, and should be converted, and I should heal them.

Matthew 13:23 But he that received seed into the good ground is he that <u>heareth the word,</u> and **understandeth *it*;** which also beareth fruit, and bringeth forth, some an hundredfold, some sixty, some thirty.

Acts 8:30 And Philip ran thither to him, and heard him read the prophet Esaias, and said, **Understandest thou what thou readest? 31** And he said, How can I, except some man should guide me? And he desired Philip that he would come up and sit with him.

c. Repent or genuinely change his mind and correct his thinking

(Please see this author's book on "How to Study the Bible for Yourself." In this book is a detailed study on "Repentance.")

Luke 13:3 I tell you, Nay: but, except ye **repent**, ye shall all likewise perish.

Luke 13:5 I tell you, Nay: but, except ye **repent**, ye shall all likewise perish.

Matthew 3:2 And saying, **Repent** ye: for the kingdom of heaven is at hand.

Matthew 4:17 From that time Jesus began to preach, and to say, **Repent**: for the kingdom of heaven is at hand.

Matthew 9:13 But go ye and learn what that meaneth, I will have mercy, and not sacrifice: for I am not come to call the righteous, but sinners to **repentance**.

Matthew 21:32 For John came unto you in the way of righteousness, and ye believed him not: but the publicans and the harlots believed him: and ye, when ye had seen it, **repented** not afterward, that ye might believe him.

Mark 1:15 And saying, The time is fulfilled, and the kingdom of God is at hand: **repent** ye, and believe the gospel.

Mark 2:17 When Jesus heard it, he saith unto them, They that are whole have no need of the physician, but they that are sick: I came not to call the righteous, but sinners to **repentance**.

Acts 20:21 Testifying both to the Jews, and also to the Greeks, **repentance** toward God, and faith toward our Lord Jesus Christ.

2 Timothy 2:25 In meekness instructing those that oppose themselves; if God peradventure will give them **repentance** to the acknowledging of the truth;

2 Peter 3:9 The Lord is not slack concerning his promise, as some men count slackness; but is longsuffering to us-ward, not willing that any should perish, but that all should come to **repentance**.

d. Believe the gospel

Mark 1:15 And saying, The time is fulfilled, and the kingdom of God is at hand: repent ye, and **believe the gospel**.

1 Corinthians 15:1 Moreover, brethren, **I declare unto you the gospel** which I preached unto you, which also ye have received, and wherein ye stand; **2 By which also ye are saved**, if ye keep in memory what I preached unto you, unless ye have believed in vain. **3** For I delivered unto you first of all that which I also received, how that **Christ died for our sins according to the scriptures**; **4** And that **he was buried**, and that **he rose again the third day according to the scriptures:**

John 3:15 That **whosoever believeth in him** should not perish, but have eternal life.

John 3:16 For God so loved the world, that he gave his only begotten Son, that **whosoever believeth in him** should not perish, but have everlasting life.

John 3:18 He that believeth on him is not condemned: but he that believeth not is condemned already, because he hath not believed in the name of the only begotten Son of God.

John 3:36 He that believeth on the Son hath everlasting life: and he that believeth not the Son shall not see life; but the wrath of God abideth on him.

John 5:24 Verily, verily, I say unto you, He that heareth my word, and believeth on him that sent me, hath everlasting life, and shall not come into condemnation; but is passed from death unto life.

John 6:47 Verily, verily, I say unto you, He that believeth on me hath everlasting life.

So, man is totally unable to pay the atonement for his own sins, but man must put his faith in Jesus and what He did on the cross to pay the atonement for his sins.

Chapter 5

<u>Unconditional Election?</u>

The Calvinist teaches that God does the electing or choosing and that it is totally unconditional on man's part. However, the Bible teaches that election or choosing is conditional. Man must choose God's way of salvation by believing the truth and trusting Christ as Savior. Study the following passages.

2 Thessalonians 2:13 But we are bound to give thanks always to God for you, brethren beloved of the Lord, because **<u>God hath from the beginning chosen you</u>** <u>to salvation through sanctification of the Spirit and</u> **<u>belief of the truth</u>**:

Titus 1:1 Paul, a servant of God, and an apostle of Jesus Christ, **<u>according to the faith of God's elect, and the acknowledging of the truth</u>** which is after godliness;

One of the things that seems to be overlooked is that God chooses man based on foreknowledge. God looks through time to see those that will choose him and those that do are in turn chosen by God and are made part of the elect. Note the following passage.

1 Peter 1:2 <u>**Elect according to the foreknowledge of God the Father**</u>, through sanctification of the Spirit, unto obedience and sprinkling of the blood of Jesus Christ: Grace unto you, and peace, be multiplied.

It has been said that **election shuts no one out but a lot of people in**. I believe that this statement is true. To make it clear the election or God choosing us for salvation is conditional. The condition is we must believe the truth and accept Christ as our Savior. God by his foreknowledge looks down through time and sees who will trust Christ as Savior and those individuals become a part of the elect.

You will notice from the very start of mankind, that God sets up Adam and Eve with a choice. God allows man to choose or reject a certain tree in the Garden of Eden. Notice the following passages of scripture.

Gen 2:9 And out of the ground made the LORD God to grow every tree that is pleasant to the sight, and good for food**; <u>the tree of life also in the midst of the garden, and the tree of knowledge of good and evil</u>**.

Gen 2:15 And the LORD God took the man, and put him into the garden of Eden to dress it and to keep it. **2:16** And the LORD God commanded the man, saying, Of every tree of the garden thou mayest freely eat: **2:17** <u>**But of the tree of the knowledge of good and evil, thou shalt not eat of it: for in the day that thou eatest thereof thou shalt surely die.**</u>

When reading the above passages of scripture, we need to remind ourselves of a couple of things. There was a special mention of two trees in verse 9. They are the Tree of Life and the Tree of the Knowledge of Good and Evil. The Tree of Life was not at this point forbidden by God to eat the fruit of it. It was only the Tree of the Knowledge of Good and Evil that God said was forbidden to eat of the fruit of that tree.

Gen 3:1 Now the serpent was more subtil than any beast of the field which the LORD God had made. And he said unto the woman, Yea, hath God said, Ye shall not eat of every tree of the garden? **3:2** And the woman said unto the serpent, **We may eat of the fruit of the trees of the garden**: **3:3** **But of the fruit of the tree which *is* in the midst of the garden, God hath said, Ye shall not eat of it, neither shall ye touch it, lest ye die.** **3:4** And the serpent said unto the woman, Ye shall not surely die: **3:5** For God doth know that in the day ye eat thereof, then your eyes shall be opened, and ye shall be as gods, knowing good and evil. **3:6** And **when the woman saw that the tree *was* good for food, and that it *was* pleasant to the eyes, and a tree to be desired to make *one* wise, she took of the fruit thereof, and did eat, and gave also unto her husband with her; and he did eat.** **3:7** And the eyes of them both were opened, and they knew that they *were* naked; and they sewed fig leaves together, and made themselves aprons. **3:8** And they heard the voice of the LORD God walking in the garden in the cool of the day: and Adam and his wife hid themselves from the presence of the LORD God amongst the trees of the garden.

In the above passage we see that Eve and then Adam chose to take of the Tree of the Knowledge of Good and Evil. We must also notice that they did not choose the Tree of Life which was not forbidden by God at the first before Adam and Eve sinned.

From this Bible story we can see that God gave Adam and Eve the ability to choose. They were not created without a freedom of choice. We must also see that it was not God's will for them to make the choice that they made. It was clearly forbidden by God. It is also important to note that Adam and Eve were not predestined to take of the forbidden fruit. Neither is mankind predestined to do all the wicked things that they do. It is a choice that we make and we will answer to God for the choices the we make, both good and bad. Mankind will also answer to God for rejecting Christ as Savior or receiving Christ. It is man's choice but it is God who will judge mankind accordingly.

It needs to be pointed out that Adam and Eve did get saved. Notice the following title given to Adam.

Luke 3:38 Which was *the son* of Enos, which was *the son* of Seth, which was *the son* of **Adam, which was *the son* of God**.

Chapter 6

Limited Atonement?

The Calvinist says Jesus only died for those who are going to believe and be saved. However, the Bible says that Jesus died for the entire human race whether they get saved or not. Please note the following passages with an explanation of for whom Jesus died.

I John 2:2 And he is the propitiation for our sins; and not for ours only, but also for the sins of the whole world.

> *Note: The above passage makes it clear that Jesus not only died for the believers as in "ours only" but also for everyone as in the "sins of the whole world." This includes those who refuse to be saved as well as those who trust Christ as their personal Savior.*

1 Timothy 4:10 For therefore we both labour and suffer reproach, because we trust in the living God, **who is the Saviour of all men, specially of those that believe**.

> *Note: The above passage makes it clear that Jesus is the Savior of all men*

which means the entire human race and then he says "especially of those that believe." This tells us that Jesus died for both those who refused to be saved as well as those who will be saved.

2Pe 2:1 But there were false prophets also among the people, even as there shall be false teachers among you, who privily shall bring in damnable heresies, **even denying the Lord that bought them**, and bring upon themselves swift destruction.

Note: The above verse tells us that Jesus even died for the false prophets and the false teachers who have obviously rejected Christ as their Savior.

1 Timothy 2:3-6 For this *is* good and acceptable in the sight of God our Saviour; **4** Who will have **all** men to be saved, and to come unto the knowledge of the truth. **5** For *there is* one God, and one mediator between God and men, the man Christ Jesus; **6** Who gave himself a ransom for **all**, to be testified in due time.

2 Peter 3:9 The Lord is not slack concerning his promise, as some men count slackness; but is longsuffering to us-ward, **not willing that any should perish**, but that **all** should come to repentance.

Hebrews 2:9 But we see Jesus, who was made a little lower than the angels for the suffering of death, crowned with glory and honour; that **he by the grace of God should taste death for every man**.

One of the events that will occur in the future for lost people or unbelievers of all ages is commonly called the "White Throne Judgment." Notice the following passage.

Revelation 20:11 And I saw a **great white throne**, and him that sat on it, from whose face the earth and the heaven fled away; and there was found no place for them. **12** And I saw **the dead**, small and great, stand before God; and the books were opened: and another book was opened, which is *the book* of life: and **the dead** were **judged** out of those things which were written in the books, according to their works. **13** And the sea gave up **the dead** which were in it; and **death and hell delivered up the dead** which were in them: and **they were judged** every man according to their works. **14** And death and hell were cast into the lake of fire. This is the second death. **15** And whosoever was not found written in the book of life was cast into the lake of fire.

Please understand first that the White Throne Judgment does not occur to see if the individuals will go to Heaven or Hell. They are already condemned to Hell because of dying in their sins before they trusted

Christ as their Savior. In light of this passage and this judgment, this brings up a lot of questions and situations that need to be addressed if we are to take the view of the Calvinist. One by one each lost person that appears at this judgment will face God but actually will have one of the greatest reasons for being at this judgment. They can tell Jesus that he did not die for them. They were predestined to be there.

That being said, **if they are predestined to Hell why bother with a judgment for them at all?** In the Bible perspective, the lost people are at this judgment because they rejected Christ as their Savior and God is there determining by their unbelief and their sins how bad their part in the lake of fire would be.

In the perspective of the Calvinist these lost people had no choice. They were not saved because they could not get saved. They were predestined to Hell so again, why bother with a judgment at all? If they are here judged for their life's sins, you have to wonder how good does anyone expect unsaved people to be if we are going to take the view of a Calvinist? **<u>God does not judge mankind on what he cannot do, but on what mankind will not do.</u>**

It needs to be understood that there are different degrees of punishment for lost people in Hell. This is another reason for the White Throne Judgment. It is to determine what will be their part in the Lake of Fire. Because the lost sinner has rejected Christ as Savior, every sin that they have ever committed will be judged at this judgment. *Please see this author's book on "A Study on Baptism and a Study on Hell."* Please notice the following.

2 Thessalonians 1:8 <u>In flaming fire taking vengeance on them that know not God, and that obey not the gospel of our Lord Jesus Christ</u>: **9 <u>Who shall be punished with everlasting destruction from the presence of the Lord, and from the glory of his power</u>**;

There are different measures or degrees of hell:

A. The Lowest Hell

> **Deuteronomy 32:22** For a fire is kindled in mine anger, and **shall burn unto the lowest hell,** and shall consume the earth with her increase, and set on fire the foundations of the mountains.

> **Psalm 86:13** For great *is* thy mercy toward me: and thou hast delivered my soul from **the lowest hell**.

B. Depths of Hell

> **Proverbs 9:18** But he knoweth not that the dead *are* there; *and that* her guests *are* in **the depths of hell**.

C. The Greater Damnation

Matthew 23:14 Woe unto you, scribes and Pharisees, hypocrites! For ye devour widows' houses, and for a pretense make long prayer: therefore ye shall receive **the greater damnation.**

Mark 12:40 Which devour widows' houses, and for a pretense make long prayers: these shall receive **greater damnation**.

Luke 20:47 Which devour widows' houses, and for a shew make long prayers: the same shall **receive greater damnation**.

D. Twofold more the Child of Hell than Yourselves

Matthew 23:15 Woe unto you, scribes and Pharisees, hypocrites! For ye compass sea and land to make one proselyte, and when he is made, ye make him **twofold more the child of hell than yourselves.**

E. Their Part in the Lake Which Burns with Fire and Brimstone

Revelation 21:8 But the fearful, and unbelieving, and the abominable, and murderers, and whoremongers, and sorcerers, and idolaters, and all liars, shall have **their part in the lake which burneth with fire and brimstone**: which is the second death.

Due to the misunderstanding of the strength and purpose of Jesus dying on the cross, it will do us well to go to the Bible and read over some verses on why Jesus died. Let us review some of the many passages in the Bible that tell us why Jesus died on the cross. This will reinforce God's testimony about how much **God loves the entire human race**. As Jesus said concerning His love for us in the following verse. **John 15:13** Greater love hath no man than this, that a man lay down his life for his friends.

> **Matthew 1:21** And she shall bring forth a son, and thou shalt call his name JESUS: for **he shall save his people from their sins.**
>
> **Matthew 18:11** For **the Son of man is come to save that which was lost**.
>
> **Matthew 20:28** Even as **the Son of man came** not to be ministered unto, but to minister, and **to give his life a ransom for many.**
>
> **Mark 10:45** For even **the Son of man came** not to be ministered unto, but to

---

minister, and **to give his life a ransom for many.**

Luke 9:56 For the **Son of man is not come to destroy men's lives, but to save _them_**. And they went to another village.

Romans 4:24 But for us also, to whom it shall be imputed, if we believe on him that raised up **Jesus our Lord** from the dead; **25 Who was delivered for our offences, and was raised again for our justification**.

Romans 5:6 For when we were yet without strength, in due time **Christ died for the ungodly**.

Romans 5:8 But God commendeth his love toward us, in that, while we were yet sinners, **Christ died for us.**

Romans 8:32 He that spared not his own Son, but **delivered him up for us all**, how shall he not with him also freely give us all things?

2 Corinthians 5:18 And all things *are* of **God, who hath reconciled us to**

himself by Jesus Christ, and hath given to us the ministry of reconciliation; **19** To wit, that **God was in Christ, reconciling the world unto himself**, not imputing their trespasses unto them; and hath committed unto us the word of reconciliation. **20** Now then we are ambassadors for Christ, as though God did beseech *you* by us: we pray *you* in Christ's stead, be ye reconciled to God. **21** For **he hath made him *to be* sin for us**, who knew no sin; that we might be made the righteousness of God in him.

Galatians 1:3 Grace *be* to you and peace from God the Father, and *from* **our Lord Jesus Christ**, **1:4 Who gave himself for our sins**, that he might deliver us from this present evil world, according to the will of God and our Father:

Galatians 3:13 Christ hath redeemed us from the curse of the law, being made a curse for us: for it is written, Cursed *is* every one that hangeth on a tree:

Ephesians 5:2 And walk in love, as **Christ also hath loved us, and hath given himself for us an offering and**

a sacrifice to God for a sweetsmelling savour.

1 Thessalonians 1:10 And to wait for his Son from heaven, whom he raised from the dead, *even* **Jesus, which delivered us from the wrath to come**.

1 Thessalonians 5:9 For God hath not appointed us to wrath, but to obtain salvation by our Lord Jesus Christ, 10 Who died for us, that, whether we wake or sleep, we should live together with him.

1 Timothy 1:15 This *is* a faithful saying, and worthy of all acceptation, that **Christ Jesus came into the world to save sinners;** of whom I am chief.

1 Timothy 2:5 For *there is* one God, and one mediator between God and men, **the man Christ Jesus; 2:6 Who gave himself a ransom for all**, to be testified in due time.

Titus 2:13 Looking for that blessed hope, and the glorious appearing of the great God and our **Saviour Jesus Christ**; **14 Who gave himself for us, that he**

might redeem us from all iniquity, and purify unto himself a peculiar people, zealous of good works.

Hebrews 1:3 Who being the brightness of *his* glory, and the express image of his person, and upholding all things by the word of his power, when **he had by himself purged our sins**, sat down on the right hand of the Majesty on high;

Hebrews 2:9 But we see Jesus, who was made a little lower than the angels for the suffering of death, crowned with glory and honour; that **he by the grace of God should taste death for every man.**

Hebrews 2:17 Wherefore in all things it behoved him to be made like unto *his* brethren, that he might be a merciful and faithful high priest in things *pertaining* to God, **to make reconciliation for the sins of the people.**

Hebrews 9:12 Neither by the blood of goats and calves, but **by his own blood he entered in once into the holy place, having obtained eternal redemption** *for us*.

Hebrews 9:26 For then must he often have suffered since the foundation of the world: but now once in the end of the world <u>**hath he appeared to put away sin by the sacrifice of himself**</u>.

Hebrews 9:28 So <u>**Christ was once offered to bear the sins of many**</u>; and unto them that look for him shall he appear the second time without sin unto salvation.

Hebrews 10:10 By the which will <u>**we are sanctified through the offering of the body of Jesus Christ once *for all*.**</u> **11** And every priest standeth daily ministering and offering oftentimes the same sacrifices, which can never take away sins: **12** But this man, after <u>**he had offered one sacrifice for sins for ever**</u>, sat down on the right hand of God;

1 Peter 2:24 <u>**Who his own self bare our sins in his own body on the tree**</u>, that we, being dead to sins, should live unto righteousness: by whose stripes ye were healed.

1 Peter 3:18 <u>**For Christ also hath once suffered for sins, the just for**</u>

the unjust, that he might bring us to God, being put to death in the flesh, but quickened by the Spirit:

1 John 2:2 And **he is the propitiation for our sins: and not for ours only, but also for *the sins of* the whole world.**

1 John 3:16 Hereby perceive we the love *of God*, because **he laid down his life for us**: and we ought to lay down *our* lives for the brethren.

1 John 4:10 Herein is love, not that we loved God, but that **he loved us, and sent his Son *to be* the propitiation for our sins.**

1 John 4:14 And we have seen and do testify that **the Father sent the Son *to be* the Saviour of the world.**

Isaiah 53:5 But **he *was* wounded for our transgressions, *he was* bruised for our iniquities**: the chastisement of our peace *was* upon him; and with his stripes we are healed. **6** All we like sheep have gone astray; we have turned every one to his own way; and **the LORD hath laid on him the iniquity of us all.**

Isaiah 53:8 He was taken from prison and from judgment: and who shall declare his generation? for he was cut off out of the land of the living: **for the transgression of my people was he stricken.**

Isaiah 53:10 Yet **it pleased the LORD to bruise him**; he hath put *him* to grief: when **thou shalt make his soul an offering for sin**, he shall see *his* seed, he shall prolong *his* days, and the pleasure of the LORD shall prosper in his hand. **11 He shall see of the travail of his soul, *and* shall be satisfied:** by his knowledge shall my righteous servant justify many; **for he shall bear their iniquities. 12** Therefore will I divide him *a portion* with the great, and he shall divide the spoil with the strong; because he hath poured out his soul unto death: and he was numbered with the transgressors; and **he bare the sin of many**, and made intercession for the transgressors.

So, we must understand according to the Bible there is no limit to the atonement that Jesus provided when He died on the cross. Even though Jesus died for every human being, it is important to keep in mind that this does not mean that every human being is automatically going to Heaven. Each individual must trust Christ and what He did for them on the cross in order to get to Heaven. Please review chapter 1.

So, remember that **Jesus died on the cross for every human being sufficiently but only effectively for those who will trust Christ as their personal Savior.**

Chapter 7

<u>Irresistible Grace?</u>

The Calvinist says that when God wants to save someone, they will be so overwhelmed by the grace of God that they will not be able to say no to God and resist God's grace and call to salvation. God will literally over power their will. They say when God saves a person, that person has no choice in the matter. It is true that if any man gets saved, he is saved by the grace of God. Note the following verses:

Ephesians 2:8 For <u>**by grace are ye saved through faith**</u>; and that not of yourselves: *it is* the gift of God: **9** Not of works, lest any man should boast.

Acts 15:11 But <u>**we believe that through the grace of the Lord Jesus Christ we shall be saved, even as they.**</u>

Romans 3:24 <u>**Being justified freely by his grace**</u> through the redemption that is in Christ Jesus:

Romans 4:16 <u>**Therefore *it is* of faith, that *it might be* by grace**</u>; to the end the promise might be sure to all the seed; not to that only which is of the law, but to that also which is of the faith of Abraham; who is the father of us all,

Romans 11:6 <u>**And if by grace, then** *is it* **no more of works**</u>: otherwise grace is no more grace. But if *it be* of works, then is it no more grace: otherwise work is no more work.

Ephesians 2:5 Even when we were dead in sins, hath quickened us together with Christ, (<u>**by grace ye are saved**</u>;)

Please understand that this marvelous grace of God at no time overrides the will of man when it comes to salvation. There are countless times where God called to man and man resisted and said no to God. The Jews resisted God's call. See the following passages.

Acts 7:51 Ye stiffnecked and uncircumcised in heart and ears, <u>ye do always **resist** the Holy Ghost: **as your fathers** *did*, **so** *do* **ye**</u>.

Matt 23:37 O Jerusalem, Jerusalem, *thou* that killest the prophets, and stonest them which are sent unto thee, <u>**how often would I have gathered thy children together, even as a hen gathereth her chickens under** *her* **wings, and ye would not!**</u>

Luke 13:34 O Jerusalem, Jerusalem, which killest the prophets, and stonest them that are sent unto thee; <u>**how often would I have gathered thy children together, as a hen** *doth gather* **her brood under** *her* **wings, and ye would not!**</u>

If it is true about God having irresistible grace and God overrides the will of man, the Bible could not say "many are called, but few chosen." **The number called would have to be the same as the number chosen.**

The truth is many are called but due to the rebellion of unbelief in man, few of the many answer the call of salvation and so few are chosen.

Matthew 20:16 So the last shall be first, and the first last: for **many be called, but few chosen.**

Matthew 22:14 For **many are called, but few *are* chosen**.

Isaiah 55:6 Seek ye the LORD while he may be found, **call ye upon him while he is near**:

Proverbs 1:24 Because I have called, and ye refused; **I have stretched out my hand, and no man regarded; 25** But ye have set at nought all my counsel, and would none of my reproof: **26** I also will laugh at your calamity; I will mock when your fear cometh; **27** When your fear cometh as desolation, and your destruction cometh as a whirlwind; when distress and anguish cometh upon you. **28 Then shall they call upon me, but I will not answer**; **they shall seek me early, but they shall not find me**: **29** For that they hated knowledge, and did not choose the fear of the LORD: **30** They would none of my counsel: they despised all my reproof. **31** Therefore shall they eat of the fruit of their own way, and be filled with their own devices.

God has shown us in the Bible that there are three access doors or switches into God's amazing grace. All three must be accessed at the same time.

The one is **faith**. Study the following passage of scripture.

Romans 5:2 By whom also <u>we have access by faith into this grace</u> wherein we stand, and rejoice in hope of the glory of God.

Another is **humility**.

James 4:6 But he giveth more grace. Wherefore he saith, God resisteth the proud, but <u>giveth grace unto the humble</u>.

1 Peter 5:5 Likewise, ye younger, submit yourselves unto the elder. Yea, all of you be subject one to another, and be clothed with humility: for <u>**God resisteth the proud, and giveth grace to the humble**</u>.

The third is **prayer** or calling on God for salvation.

Hebrews 4:16 Let us therefore come boldly unto the throne of grace, that we may obtain mercy, and find grace to help in time of need.

Romans 10:13 For whosoever shall call upon the name of the Lord shall be saved.

So, faith or believing God's word and what it says about how to be saved is required. We must humble ourselves before God seeing ourselves as Hell deserving sinners. Then we must with desire from our hearts call on Jesus to save our souls. This gives us access to this amazing grace. Notice the good works or good deeds or obedience to God's commands cannot give us access to God's grace. So as amazing as God's grace is it will never override the will of man concerning the salvation of his soul.

Rom 11:6 And if by grace, then *is it* no more of works: otherwise grace is no more grace. But if *it be* of works, then is it no more grace: otherwise work is no more work.

Chapter 8

Perseverance of the Saints?

The Calvinist says we are eternally saved because saved man will persevere and endure to the end.

The Bible says we are eternally saved by God's grace, but it is because God hangs on to us. It is not because we are trying to hang on to God. Please see this author's book on "Eternal Security."

Jude 24 Now unto him that is able to keep you from falling, and to present *you* faultless before the presence of his glory with exceeding joy,

Again, salvation is eternal because God hangs on to us and not because we hang on God. Notice the following:

John 10:28–29 And I give unto them eternal life; and they shall never perish, **neither shall any *man* pluck them out of my hand**. **29** My Father, which gave *them* me, is greater than all; and **no *man* is able to pluck *them* out of my Father's hand**.

Ps 37:23 The steps of a *good* man are ordered by the LORD: and he delighteth in his way.
Ps 37:24 Though he fall, he shall not be utterly cast down: **for the LORD upholdeth *him with* his hand.**

Remember it is God who is hanging on to us and not us who are hanging on to God. Perhaps the following illustration will help with this point.

Remember as an adult you have taken your children when they were small and just learning how to walk and together you go out for a stroll. They would try to hang on to your hand but when they stumble, they would lose their grip and fall.

However, if you as an adult would hang on to their hand, the only way they would fall is for you to fall. The only way a true believer will fall is for God to fall and that is impossible. God will not let go of His grip and you are not going to fall or lose your salvation.

There is a misunderstanding of the expression used in the Bible. The expression is "enduring to the end." Notice the following passages.

Matt 10:22 And ye shall be hated of all *men* for my name's sake: but **he that endureth to the end shall be saved**.

Matt 24:13 But he that shall **endure unto the end, the same shall be saved**.

Mark 13:13 And ye shall be hated of all *men* for my name's sake: but he that shall **endure unto the end, the same shall be saved.**

The enduring to the end mentioned in the passages above is referring to saving their natural lives and not referring to the saving of their souls.

See the following passages that follow the above passages mentioned.

Matt 24:22 And except those days should be shortened, **there should no flesh be saved**: but for the elect's sake those days shall be shortened.

Mark 13:20 And except that the Lord had shortened those days**, no flesh should be saved**: but for the elect's sake, whom he hath chosen, he hath shortened the days.

The saving due to the endurance is referring to the natural life of the believer as in the phrase "no flesh should be saved." It is not reference to the salvation of the soul. The salvation of the soul is instant.

So again remember, **it is God hanging on to us and not us hanging on to God.**

Chapter 9

Predestination

First an Explanation of a Sample of What I Call a "Word Study Sentence"

Most software Bible programs can produce these word study sentences at the stroke of a few keys. Note the following example:

Note: The word "**study**" in II Tim. 2:15 #4704 (11x)(endeavour-3; do diligence-2; be diligent-2; give diligence; be forward; **labour**; study)

First allow me to explain each part of the word study sentence. "Study" is the word in question that is being looked up. The next part is the Strong's number for that word which represents the Greek word for the word "study" which is **#4704**. It is Greek because the word in question is in the New Testament. **The use of a Strong's Concordance is required**. Simply look up the word "study" in the Strong's just like you would look up a word in a dictionary. After finding the word "study" in the Strong's, you can see below the word and to the left in the New Testament reference which is II Timothy 2:15. To the right on the same line you can see the Strong's number **#4704**. With "**The New Strong's Expanded Dictionary of Bible Words**" you can produce the following information. The next part in the word study sentence is the number followed by an "x" which is how many times that (#4704) appears in the New Testament. It appears 11 times. Next are the different ways the (#4704) are translated in the King James Bible followed by the number of times each word appears in the New Testament. These different English translations, because of the preservation of both the English and Greek produce synonyms and definitions for the word "STUDY." There is not only computer software available to produce this word study sentence, but also other hard copy books out that can give you the same information.

Now let's do a study on the word "predestination" and its doctrine. First notice the word study sentence below on the word. "predestination."

Predestination: (#4309) **proorizo** (6x)(determine before-1; ordain-1; predestinate-4)

So, the word "Predestination" appears 6 times in the Bible and only in the New Testament. As you look farther down the sentence we can see the different ways that the Greek word,"Proorizo," is translated into English.

Next notice that the Greek word "proorizo" is a compound word and now notice the two words put together that make up the word, predestination. They are "pro" and "horizo." The word study sentence for both are below.

> [**pro** (#4253)(50x)(translated 44 times "**before**"; above-3; ago; began; or ever)
>
> **horizo**- (#3724)(8x)(translated ordained-2; determined-3; declared; determinate; limiteth]

So, the definition of "predestination" is that God predetermines that something will and must happen before it actually does.

Keep in mind that according to **Rom. 8:29** predestination is based on God's foreknowledge. Now notice the total list of verses on predestination. To keep things in perspective there are only 6 verses in the whole Bible on "Predestination." This flies up in the face of the individuals who think everything is predested.

> **Acts 4:28** For to do whatsoever thy hand and thy counsel **determined before #4309** to be done.
>
> **Rom. 8:29** For whom he did foreknow, he also did **predestinate #4309** to be conformed to the image of his Son, that he might be the firstborn among many brethren.

Rom. 8:30 Moreover whom he did **predestinate #4309**, them he also called: and whom he called, them he also justified: and whom he justified, them he also glorified.

I Cor. 2:7 But we speak the wisdom of God in a mystery, even the hidden wisdom, which God **ordained before #4309** the world unto our glory.

Eph. 1:5 Having **predestinated #4309** us unto the adoption of children by Jesus Christ to himself, according to the good pleasure of his will,

Eph. 1:11 In whom also we have obtained an inheritance, being **predestinated #4309** according to the purpose of him who worketh all things after the counsel of his own will:

From the above six verses in the Bible there is a total of only **five things mentioned in the Bible that are predestined**. It is a sad mistake to assume that everything in life is predestined. It is not a case of whatever will be will be. This would mean that God predestined sin, the fall of man, and the condemnation of man to Hell just to name a few. This would make life already set in stone with all the events locked in place. The details of our future in this life have not been predetermined or written yet. Man has the liberty and responsibility to choose his future steps. Not everything is determined beforehand by God, according to the Bible. The following things are determined beforehand or predestinated by God.

1) The Believer's Adoption

> **Eph. 1:5** Having **predestinated #4309** us unto the **adoption** of children by Jesus Christ to himself, according to the good pleasure of his will,

2) The Believer's Inheritance

> **Eph. 1:11** In whom also we have **obtained an inheritance**, being **predestinated #4309** according to the purpose of him who worketh all things after the counsel of his own will:

3) The Believer to be Conformed into the image of Christ

> **Rom. 8:29** For whom he did foreknow, he also did **predestinate #4309** to be **conformed to the image of his Son**, that he might be the firstborn among many brethren.

These first three things that predestination applies to are to the believer only. To be a believer is not predestined. Once a person trusts Christ as their personal Savior then their adoption, inheritance, and being conformed into the image of Christ are all predestinated.

4) The wisdom of God and Prophesy written in the Word of God

> **I Cor. 2:7** But we speak the wisdom of God in a mystery, even the hidden wisdom, which God **ordained before #4309** the world unto our glory.

Psalm 119:89 For ever, O LORD, thy word is settled in heaven.

So, the Bible and its prophesy are predestinated and settled in heaven. What the Bible says in prophecy will come to pass and is unstoppable and unavoidable.

5) The Crucifixion of Christ

Acts 4:26 The kings of the earth stood up, and the rulers were gathered together against the Lord, and against his Christ. **27** For of a truth against thy holy child Jesus, whom thou hast anointed, both Herod, and Pontius Pilate, with the Gentiles, and the people of Israel, were gathered together, **28** For to do whatsoever thy hand and thy counsel **determined before #4309** to be done.

Finally, the crucifixion is predestined by God and could not be stopped.

Since Predestination is based on foreknowledge, God looked down through time and saw that man would sin and rebel and be in need of a perfect atonement and sacrifice for man's sins. That would of course be Jesus. **The predestination of God does not destroy the free agency of man or lighten the responsibility of the lost sinner to trust Christ.**

Revelation 13:8 And all that dwell upon the earth shall worship him *(the beast)*, whose names are not written in the book of life of **the Lamb slain from the foundation of the world**.

1 Peter 1:18 Forasmuch as ye know that ye were not redeemed with corruptible things, *as* silver and gold, from your vain conversation *received* by tradition from your fathers; **19** But with the **precious blood of Christ, as of a lamb without blemish and without spot**: **20 Who verily was foreordained before the foundation of the world,** but was manifest in these last times for you,

After reviewing the five things in the Bible that are predestinated, this leaves countless things that are not predestinated. We must realize that everything that happens is not predestined by God. Allow me to name a few things that are not predestined. Where man spends eternity is not predestinated. The believers' inheritance is predestined. The believers' adoption is predestined, and the believers' conformation into the image of Christ is predestined. However, for man to be a believer is not predestinated. Each person must first trust Christ as their Savior. Each person has the right and responsibility to choose and trust Christ. Man sinning against God is not predestinated. God in His foreknowledge saw the sin of man coming but it was not predestinated.

Just because God sees something coming in the future does not mean it is God's fault or God's will that it comes. For example, Jesus saw that Peter was going to deny Him three times and even told him in advance, but it was not God's fault or God's will that Peter should deny Christ. Even though Jesus told Peter that he would do it, Peter made that choice himself and had to face the consequences of denying Christ.

This would be a good place to bring up the subject of Calvinism versus hyper-Calvinism. The Calvinist declares that some individuals are predestined for heaven. However, they deny what they call double predestination. This phrase came about by the "hyper-Calvinist" who believes in double predestination. They believe that some people are predestinated to heaven and the rest are predestinated to Hell. The hyper-Calvinist actually reveals a weak point that the anti-Calvinist has made for centuries. The point is if you are going to believe like the Calvinist, that some people are predestined for heaven, you are going to also have to believe that some people are predestined for hell. This exposes the ugly and dangerous doctrine of Calvinism.

Chapter 10

<u>Adoption</u>

One of the common errors made by many is to confuse adoption with salvation. Salvation is instant upon trusting Christ as Savior and Adoption is future for the one that has trusted Christ as their Savior. Now, let us get into the study from the Bible on adoption.

Notice the word study sentence for the word "adoption."

Adoption #5206 (5x)(adoption-5)

As you can see, there are 5 places in the Bible where the word, "adoption," appears and all of them appear in the New Testament. There are no other English words used in the Bible for #5206 but the word, adoption.

Now notice the word "adoption" in the Greek is a compound word. It is "huiothesia." The first part is "huios" and the second part is "theso." Now notice the word study sentences for both of these words from the compound word below.

> [huios-#5207   (382x)(translated   as child-3; children-47, son-307, sons-24 or foal)

[theso-#5087 (98x) From the many English words translated in the KJV from this Greek word here are a few: (make-6; made-3; appointed-4; appoint-2; ordained-2)

Putting the two together would define "adoption" as "son appointed." Adoption is also defined in the Bible as the glorification of the believer's body which is the final completion of his redemption. The salvation of man's soul is instant upon trusting Christ as Savior but his body will not be glorified until later in the future. At that time the adoption of the believer is complete when the believer is glorified. You will see this more in the study below.

The following are passages on the subject of adoption. Again, to keep things in perspective there are only five verses in the whole Bible on the word, "adoption."

Rom. 8:15 For ye have not received the spirit of bondage again to fear; but ye have received the Spirit of **adoption**, whereby we cry, Abba, Father.
Note: The believer has received already the Spirit of adoption but not yet the adoption itself. Remember is it future for the believer.

Rom. 8:23 And not only they, but ourselves also, which have the firstfruits of the Spirit, even we ourselves groan within ourselves, <u>waiting for **adoption,** to wit, the redemption of our body</u>.

Note: This passage makes it clear that the adoption is for the believer and it is future. This is why we are told to wait for the adoption. This passage also defines the believer's adoption as "the redemption of our body." At this point the believer is glorified, complete with a glorified body, soul, and spirit and with no sinful nature.

Rom. 9:4 Who are Israelites; to whom pertaineth the **adoption**, and the glory, and the covenants, and the giving of the law, and the service of God, and the promises;

Gal. 4:5 To redeem them that were under the law, that we <u>might receive</u> the **adoption** of sons.

Note: "might receive the adoption" is future and is promised to come but is yet to come.

Eph. 1:5 Having predestinated us unto the **adoption** of children by Jesus Christ to himself, according to the good pleasure of his will,

*Adoption is future and for the believer only. **(Rom. 8:23; Gal. 4:5)** and according to **Eph. 1:5** the adoption is predestinated for the believer. A word of warning needs to be inserted here again not to confuse "adoption" with "salvation." Salvation occurs immediately upon trusting Christ as Savior and the adoption for the believer comes when the believer is glorified.*

1 John 3:2 Beloved, **now are we the sons of God**, and it doth not yet appear what we shall be: but we know that, when he shall appear, we shall be like him; for we shall see him as he is.

The "adoption" occurs in the believer's future when we receive a glorified body. The believer presently has the spirit of adoption but not yet the adoption itself. ***(Rom. 8:15)***

Chapter 11

Foreknowledge

*Foreknowledge is an attribute of
God and not an act of God.*

God knowing something bad will happen in the future does not make it his fault that it happens. Allow me to warn you not to confuse foreknowledge with predestination. Repeating the example previously stated, Peter denies Jesus three times. Jesus knew the denial was coming and warned Peter that it would, but it was not Jesus' fault that Peter did it and Peter was not predestined to do it. Peter chose to do it and God saw it coming but it was not God's will that he should deny Him. Notice the following scripture.

An Example of Jesus' Foreknowledge of Peter's Denial

Mark 14:30 And Jesus saith unto him, Verily I say unto thee, That this day, even in this night, **before the cock crow twice, thou shalt deny me thrice**.

Now Peter's Denial

Mark 14:67 And when she saw Peter warming himself, she looked upon him, and said, And thou also wast with Jesus of Nazareth. **68** But **he denied**, saying, I know not, neither understand I what thou sayest. And he went out into the porch; and the cock crew. **69** And a maid saw him again, and began to say to them that stood by, This is one of them. **70** And <u>he denied it again</u>. And a little after, they that stood by said again to Peter, Surely thou art one of them: for thou art a Galilaean, and thy speech agreeth thereto. **71** But he began to curse and to swear, saying, I know not this man of whom ye speak. **72** And the second time the cock crew. And <u>**Peter called to mind the word that Jesus said unto him, Before the cock crow twice, thou shalt deny me thrice**</u>. And when he thought thereon, he wept.

No English form of the word "foreknowledge" appears in the Old Testament but there are two Greek words for some form of the word "foreknowledge" in the New Testament. Their Strong's #'s are #4267 and #4268. Now notice the word study sentences and the scripture references for the word "foreknowledge."

The following is the first Greek word.

> **(#4267)** proginosko (5x)(foreknow-2; foreordain; know; know before)

Now breaking the compound word "proginosko" into two words we have the following.

> pro-#4253 (50x)(translated as **before**-44; above-3; ago; began; or ever)

ginosko-#1097 (224x)(Of the many English translations from this Greek word, some form of the English word "**know**" appears 192 times)

So, putting these two words together we come up with the phrase, "know before."

Now notice the following passages in the Bible using the Greek word, "foreknowledge."

Acts 26:5 Which **knew** me **from the beginning #4267**, if they would testify, that after the most straitest sect of our religion I lived a Pharisee.

Rom. 8:29 For whom he **did foreknow #4267**, he also did predestinate to be conformed to the image of his Son, that he might be the firstborn among many brethren.

Romans 11:2 God hath not cast away his people which he **foreknew #4267**. Wot ye not what the scripture saith of Elias? how he maketh intercession to God against Israel, saying,

I Pet. 1:20 Who verily was **foreordained #4267** before the foundation of the world, but was manifest in these last times for you.

2 Peter 3:17 Ye therefore, beloved, seeing ye **know *these things* before #4267**, beware lest ye also, being led away with the error of the wicked, fall from your own stedfastness.

Now notice the second Greek word and word study sentence on the word "foreknowledge."

(#4268) Prognosis (2x)(foreknowledge-2)

You have heard doctors use this word when referring to the illness of a patient. They would give you're their prognosis. To the human doctor it would be an educated guess but God knows exactly what is going to happen in the future.

Acts 2:23 Him, being delivered by the determinate counsel and **foreknowledge** of God, ye have taken, and by wicked hands have crucified and slain:

I Pet. 1:2 Elect according to the **foreknowledge** of God the Father, through sanctification of the Spirit, unto obedience and sprinkling of the blood of Jesus Christ, Grace unto you, and peace, be multiplied.

Please allow me to reemphasize that it must be understood that God's foreknowledge is an attribute of God not an act of God. Foreknowledge is not the same as God taking actions and what He will do or not do. As has already been mentioned, Jesus knowing that Peter was about to deny Him three times, did not cause Jesus to stop him even though Jesus warned Peter and neither was it Jesus' fault or His will that Peter denied Christ. Now consider another passage in the Bible that again proves that God's foreknowledge is entirely different form His taking action.

Matthew 11:21 Woe unto thee, Chorazin! woe unto thee, Bethsaida! for <u>if the mighty works, which were done in you, had been done in Tyre and Sidon, they would have repented long ago in sackcloth and ashes.</u>

When a statement is made like this, we can see that the foreknowledge of God and His action are not the same. From the above verse we can see the foreknowledge of God in the phrase "if the mighty works, which were done in you, had been done in Tyre and Sidon, they would have repented." However, we also see that God restrained any action on Tyre and Sidon like the action on Chorazin and Bethsaida. With this statement "they would have repented" makes it clear that even though God wants everyone saved, He again will not interfere with the lost sinner's own free will even though God's own foreknowledge tells Him what will happen by man rejecting God.

Realizing that God knows in advance who will go to Heaven and who will go to Hell, this does bring up questions that need to be dealt with at this point. Does everyone have a chance to be saved before they die? What about people who have never heard the gospel? Since God can see ahead on who will be saved and who will be lost, is it possible that everyone is given a chance to be saved? Be aware that arguments will arise against the truth that Jesus is the only way to heaven and the truth that no one is predestined to Hell.

On the one hand there are those that want to say that there has to be more than one way to heaven besides Jesus, because not everyone will hear about Jesus before they die. On the other hand, if God knows in advance who will be lost or saved how is it not determined in advance or predestined by God on who will go to Hell? With this being said, first of all please understand that every human that has and will ever exist has a chance to be saved. God loves us all. Allow me to illustrate with the passages below.

Matthew 10:29 *Are not two sparrows sold for a farthing? and **one of them shall not fall on the ground without your Father.***

Luke 12:6 *Are not five sparrows sold for two farthings, and **not one of them is forgotten before God?** 7 But even the very hairs of your head are all numbered. Fear not therefore: ye are of more value than many sparrows.*

From these verses God makes it clear that no sparrow falls on the ground without our heavenly Father. God does not let even one sparrow slip through his fingers and not one of the sparrows is forgotten by God. So that being true, you have to believe that God is not going to let one human made in the image of God die without a chance at receiving the gospel. Like Jesus said, we are of more value than many sparrows. Now let's study the passages below very carefully.

John 1:9 <u>*That*</u> <u>was the true Light, which</u> **<u>lighteth</u>** **<u>every man that cometh into the world</u>**.
Please notice the phrase "lighteth every man."

Colossians 1:5 For the hope which is laid up for you in heaven, whereof ye heard before in **<u>the word of the</u>** **<u>truth of the gospel</u>**; **6** **<u>Which is come unto you, as</u>** ***<u>it</u>*** ***<u>is</u>*** **<u>in all the world</u>**; and bringeth forth fruit, as *it doth* also in you, since the day ye heard *of it*, and knew the grace of God in truth:

Colossians 1:23 If ye continue in the faith grounded and settled, and *be* not moved away from the hope of **<u>the</u>** **<u>gospel</u>**, which ye have heard, <u>*and*</u> **<u>which was preached</u>** **<u>to every creature which is under heaven</u>**; whereof I Paul am made a minister;

Titus 2:11 For the grace of God that bringeth salvation hath appeared **<u>to all men</u>**,

Psalm 98:3 He hath remembered his mercy and his truth toward the house of Israel: **<u>all the ends of the</u>** **<u>earth have seen the salvation of our God.</u>**

With the above verses in mind, allow me to break down in detail what God has done and will do for each human being. Designed by God are two witnesses that every person that has ever existed will receive to draw them to God. These witnesses are unavoidable.

The first witness is the creation itself. Just like the building declares the builder, and the painting declares the painter, so creation declares the Creator. No one can exist in creation without noticing the creation. Notice the following passage.

Psalm 19:1 The **heavens declare the glory of God**; and the firmament sheweth his handywork. **2** Day unto day uttereth speech, and night unto night sheweth knowledge. **3** ***There is* no speech nor language, *where* their voice is not heard**.

The second witness is the human conscience. This homing device given by God and undamaged also draws the individual to God. Notice the following passage.

Romans 2:15 Which shew the work of the law written in their hearts, **their conscience also bearing witness**, and *their* thoughts the mean while accusing or else excusing one another;) to get close to Him, God will see to it that that person will get the details of the gospel so that they can be saved. The following is an excellent example from the Bible of one who was longing for God and was given the details of the gospel and got saved.

Acts 10:1 There was a certain man in Caesarea called **Cornelius,** a centurion of the band called the

Italian *band*, **2** *A* devout *man*, and one that feared God with all his house, which gave much alms to the people, and prayed to God alway. **3** He saw in a vision evidently about the ninth hour of the day an angel of God coming in to him, and saying unto him, Cornelius. **4** And when he looked on him, he was afraid, and said, What is it, Lord? And he said unto him, Thy prayers and thine alms are come up for a memorial before God. **5** And now send men to Joppa, **and call for *one* Simon, whose surname is Peter**: **6** He lodgeth with one Simon a tanner, whose house is by the sea side: **he shall tell thee what thou oughtest to do.**

Now, notice in the next passage that the scripture reveals what it is that Cornelius must do and refers to a warning from God.

Acts 10:22 And they said, **Cornelius** the centurion, a just man, and one that feareth God, and of good report among all the nation of the Jews, **was warned from God by an holy angel to send for thee into his house, and to hear words of thee.**

Now, notice in the next passage that the scripture reveals what the warning actually was.

Acts 11:12 And the Spirit bade me go with them, nothing doubting. Moreover these six brethren accompanied me, and we entered into the man's house: *(Cornelius' house)* **11:13** And he shewed us how he had seen an angel in his house, which stood and said unto him, Send men to Joppa, and call for Simon, whose surname is Peter; **11:14 Who shall tell thee words, whereby thou and all thy house shall be saved.**

The warning was that Cornelius was lost and needed to be saved and God told him to send for Peter to give him the gospel.

In the next passage the Bible tells us what Peter said to Cornelius.

Acts 10:36 The word which *God* sent unto the children of Israel, preaching **peace by Jesus Christ: (he is Lord of all:) 10:37** That word, *I say*, ye know, which was published throughout all Judaea, and began from Galilee, after the baptism which John preached; **10:38** How God anointed **Jesus of Nazareth** with the Holy Ghost and with power: who went about doing good, and healing all that were oppressed of the devil; for God was with him. **10:39** And we are witnesses of all things which he did both in the land of the Jews, and in Jerusalem; whom **they slew and hanged on a tree**: **10:40 Him God raised up the third day, and shewed him openly; 10:41** Not to all the people, but unto witnesses chosen before of God, *even* to us, who did eat and drink with him **after he rose from the dead**. **10:42** And he commanded us to preach unto the people, and to testify that it is **he which was ordained of God** *to be* **the Judge of quick and dead. 10:43**

To him give all the prophets witness, that through his name whosoever believeth in him shall receive remission of sins.

If you will continue reading the story of Cornelius you will see that God sent Peter to Cornelius to give him the gospel and Cornelius got saved.

The question might be asked, what if the soul winner is unwilling to go where God sends him so the people can receive the details of the gospel? What will God do next? The story of Jonah and the whale is a good example of an unwilling soul winner that God has to bring him in line with His will to witness to a group of people.

Jonah 1:1 Now the word of the LORD came unto Jonah the son of Amittai, saying, **2** Arise, **go to Nineveh, that great city, and cry against it;** for their wickedness is come up before me. **3** But Jonah rose up to flee unto Tarshish from the presence of the LORD, and went down to Joppa; and he found a ship going to Tarshish: so he paid the fare thereof, and went down into it, to go with them unto Tarshish from the presence of the LORD.

Jonah 3:1 And the word of the LORD came unto Jonah the second time, saying, **2** Arise, **go unto Nineveh, that great city, and preach unto it the preaching that I bid thee**. **3** So Jonah arose, and went unto Nineveh, according to the word of the LORD. Now Nineveh was an exceeding great city of three days' journey.

After reading this story in the book of Jonah we see that God will go through whatever it takes to get the soul winner in place to preach the gospel to the lost. So, in conclusion, we know according to the Bible everyone has a chance before they die to get saved if they want it and no one is predestined to Hell.

Now to summarize the issue of foreknowledge, foreknowledge is simply knowing in advance that something will happen. God, who is all-wise and all-knowing, knows everything that will happen in advance. God and only God knows the future before it happens. Man, at best gives predictions and projections of what might could happen. Sad to say, many gullible human beings have been abused and taken advantage of by con-artists that claim to be able to tell them their future. Using the props of crystal balls, cards, lines in the palms of people's hands, the con-artists have made their ill-gotten gain from gullible people, some how convincing them that they know their future.

Please note the following passages about our future.

Prov 27:1 Boast not thyself of to morrow; for **thou knowest not what a day may bring forth.**

Jas 4:13 Go to now, ye that say, To day or to morrow we will go into such a city, and continue there a year, and buy and sell, and get gain: **Jas 4:14** Whereas **ye know not what *shall be* on the morrow**. For what *is* your life? It is even a vapour, that appeareth for a little time, and then vanisheth away.

Matt 6:34 Take therefore no thought for the morrow:

for the morrow shall take thought for the things of itself. Sufficient unto the day *is* the evil thereof.

In closing, foreknowledge is an attribute of God and not an attribute of man.

Chapter 12

<u>Election in the Old Testament</u>

Note: There is only 1 Hebrew word for "elect" in the Old Testament.

The word study sentence is as follows:
(#972)(13x)(chosen-8; elect-4; choose-1)

The following is a list of the 13 verses in the Old Testament that have the word "elect" in them.

2Sa 21:6 Let seven men of his sons be delivered unto us, and we will hang them up unto the LORD in Gibeah of Saul, *whom* the LORD did **choose.**[972] And the king said, I will give *them.*

1Ch 16:13 O ye seed of Israel his servant, ye children of Jacob, his **chosen ones.**[972]

Psa 89:3 I have made a covenant with my **chosen,**[972] I have sworn unto David my servant,

Psa 105:6 O ye seed of Abraham his servant, ye children of Jacob his **chosen.**[972]

Psa 105:43 And he brought forth his people with joy, *and* his **chosen**[972] with gladness:

Psa 106:5 That I may see the good of thy **chosen,**[972] that I may rejoice in the gladness of thy nation, that I may glory with thine inheritance.

Psa 106:23 Therefore he said that he would destroy them, had not Moses his **chosen**[972] stood before him in the breach, to turn away his wrath, lest he should destroy *them.*

Isa 42:1 Behold my servant, whom I uphold; mine **elect,**[972] *in whom* my soul delighteth; I have put my spirit upon him: he shall bring forth judgment to the Gentiles.

Isa 43:20 The beast of the field shall honor me, the dragons and the owls: because I give waters in the wilderness, *and* rivers in the desert, to give drink to my people, my **chosen.**[972]

Isa 45:4 For Jacob my servant's sake, and Israel mine **elect,**[972] I have even called thee by thy name: I have surnamed thee, though thou hast not known me.

Isa 65:9 And I will bring forth a seed out of Jacob, and out of Judah an inheritor of my mountains: and mine **elect**[972] shall inherit it, and my servants shall dwell there.

Isa 65:15 And ye shall leave your name for a curse unto my **chosen:**[972] for the Lord GOD shall slay thee, and call his servants by another name:

Isa 65:22 They shall not build, and another inhabit; they shall not plant, and another eat: for as the days of a tree *are* the days of my people, and mine **elect**[972] shall long enjoy the work of their hands.

From the above passages we will see the different groups of individuals that God calls His elect. They are as follows:

1. The first group is the children of Israel. (I Chron. 16:13; Psa 105:6, 43; Isa. 45:4; 65:9)

The reader must be aware that it is not automatic that the children of Israel are God's elect just because of their blood line. There is more insight to the elect of Israel given in the New Testament. Notice the following passages in the New Testament.

Rom 9:6 Not as though the word of God hath taken none effect. **For they *are* not all Israel, which are of Israel: 9:7 Neither, because they are the seed of Abraham, *are they* all children**: but, **In Isaac shall thy seed be called. 9:8** That is, **They which are the children of the flesh, these *are* not the children of God: but the children of the promise are counted for the seed.**

So, this tells us that of the children of Israel, it is those that have believed the gospel that are the chosen of Israel. Notice now another passage.

Gal 3:8 And the scripture, foreseeing that God would justify the heathen through faith, **preached before the gospel unto Abraham**, *saying*, **In thee shall all nations be blessed.**

2. The second group is referring to all believers in the future.

   Isa 43:20 The beast of the field shall honor me, the dragons and the owls: because I give waters in the wilderness, *and* rivers in the desert, to give drink to my people, my **chosen.**[972]

   Isa 65:22 They shall not build, and another inhabit; they shall not plant, and another eat: for as the days of a tree *are* the days of my people, and mine **elect**[972] shall long enjoy the work of their hands.

Also, from the passages above there are certain individuals singled out who are called God's elect. They are as follows:

1. David

   Psa 89:3 I have made a covenant with my **chosen,**[972] I have sworn unto David my servant,

2. Moses

   Psa 106:23 Therefore he said that he would destroy them, had not Moses his **chosen**[972] stood before him in the breach, to turn away his wrath, lest he should destroy *them*.

3. Jesus

Isa 42:1 Behold my servant, whom I uphold; mine **elect,**[972] *in whom* my soul delighteth; I have put my spirit upon him: he shall bring forth judgment to the Gentiles.

Chapter 13

<u>Election in the New Testament</u>

Note: There are 3 different Greek words in the New Testament for the word "election." Their numbers are as follows: #4899; #1588; and #1589 and it totals (31) passages of scripture.

Election: The true statement has been said that **election shuts no one out but a lot of people in.**

2 Thessalonians 2:13 But we are bound to give thanks alway to God for you, brethren beloved of the Lord, because **God hath from the beginning *chosen* you to salvation through sanctification of the Spirit and belief of the truth**:

Election is conditional and the condition for being part of the elect is "belief of the truth". Also, as can be seen from the passage below, election like predestination is based on foreknowledge.

1 Peter 1:2 <u>Elect</u> <u>according to the foreknowledge of God the Father</u>, through sanctification of the Spirit, unto obedience and sprinkling of the blood of Jesus Christ: Grace unto you, and peace, be multiplied.

Allow me to explain the following statement. "Election is based on foreknowledge." God is able to look into the future to see who will choose Christ and who will reject Christ. God chooses or elects individuals in the past before they exist because He knows they will choose Him in the future.

In the following we will see the three Greek #'s for the word, "elect" and the word study sentences and the scripture references.

#1 (4899)(1x)(elected together with-1)

1 Peter 5:13 The *church that is* at Babylon, **elected together with** *you*, saluteth you; and *so doth* Marcus my son.

#2 (1588)(23x)[elect-7; chosen-16]

Matthew 20:16 So the last shall be first, and the first last: **for many be called, but few chosen**.

Matthew 22:14 **For many are called, but few *are* chosen.**

Note: The above two passages prove that more are called than are chosen or elected. If the elect are already set in stone and predetermined with no condition, why would there be more called than chosen? Why would God bother calling those that are not part of the elect?

The number chosen and called would be the same according to the Calvinists.

Matthew 24:22 And except those days should be shortened, there should no flesh be saved: but for the **elect's** sake those days shall be shortened.

Matthew 24:24 For there shall arise false Christs, and false prophets, and shall shew great signs and wonders; insomuch that, if *it were* possible, they shall deceive the very **elect**.

Matthew 24:31 And he shall send his angels with a great sound of a trumpet, and they shall gather together his **elect** from the four winds, from one end of heaven to the other.

Mark 13:20 And except that the Lord had shortened those days, no flesh should be saved: but for the **elect's #1588** sake, whom he hath **chosen #1586**, he hath shortened the days.

Note: "chosen" #1586 (21x)("choose" 19x, "choose out", and "make choice")

Mark 13:22 For false Christs and false prophets shall rise, and shall shew signs and wonders, to seduce, if *it were* possible, even the **elect**.

Mark 13:27 And then shall he send his angels, and shall gather together his **elect** from the four winds, from the uttermost part of the earth to the uttermost part of heaven.

Luke 18:7 And shall not God avenge his own **elect**, which cry day and night unto him, though he bear long with them?

Luke 23:35 And the people stood beholding. And the rulers also with them derided *him*, saying, He saved others; let him save himself, if he be Christ, the **chosen** of God.

Romans 8:33 Who shall lay anything to the charge of God's **elect**? *It is* God that justifieth.

Romans 16:13 Salute Rufus **chosen** in the Lord, and his mother and mine.

Colossians 3:12 Put on therefore, as the **elect** of God, holy and beloved, bowels of mercies, kindness, humbleness of mind, meekness, longsuffering;

1 Timothy 5:21 I charge *thee* before God, and the Lord Jesus Christ, and the **elect** angels, that thou observe these things without preferring one before another, doing nothing by partiality.

II Tim. 2:10 Therefore I endure all things for the **elect's** sakes, that they may also obtain the salvation which is in Christ Jesus with eternal glory.

Titus 1:1 Paul, a servant of God, and an apostle of Jesus Christ, according to the faith of God's **elect,** and the acknowledging of the truth which is after godliness;

1 Peter 1:2 <u>**Elect** according to the foreknowledge</u> of God the Father, through sanctification of the Spirit, unto obedience and sprinkling of the blood of Jesus Christ: Grace unto you, and peace, be multiplied.

Note: God chooses us from the past because He knows by His foreknowledge that we will choose Him in the future.

1 Peter 2:4 To whom coming, *as unto* a living stone, disallowed indeed of men, but **chosen** of God, *and* precious,

1 Peter 2:6 Wherefore also it is contained in the scripture, Behold, I lay in Sion a chief corner stone, **elect**, precious: and he that believeth on him shall not be confounded.

1 Peter 2:9 But ye *are* a **chosen** generation, a royal priesthood, an holy nation, a peculiar people; that ye should shew forth the praises <u>of him who hath "called" you out of darkness into his marvellous light:</u>

2 John 1 The elder unto the **elect** lady and her children, whom I love in the truth; and not I only, but also all they that have known the truth;

2 John 13 The children of thy **elect** sister greet thee. Amen.

Revelation 17:14 These shall make war with the Lamb, and the Lamb shall overcome them: for he is Lord of lords, and King of kings: and they that are with him *are* called, and **chosen**, and faithful.

#3 (1589)(7 times) [election-6; chosen-1]

Acts 9:15 But the Lord said unto him, Go thy way: for he is a **chosen** vessel unto me, to bear my name before the Gentiles, and kings, and the children of Israel:

Rom. 9:11 (For the children being not yet born, neither having done any good or evil, that the purpose of God according to **election** might stand, not of works, but of him that calleth;)

Romans 11:5 Even so then at this present time also there is a remnant according to the **election** of grace.

Romans 11:7 What then? Israel hath not obtained that which he seeketh for; but the **election** hath obtained it, and the rest were blinded

Romans 11:28 As concerning the gospel, *they are* enemies for your sakes: but as touching the **election**, *they are* beloved for the fathers' sakes.

1 Thessalonians 1:4 Knowing, brethren beloved, your **election** of God.

2 Peter 1:10 Wherefore the rather, brethren, give diligence to make your calling and **election** sure: for if ye do these things, ye shall never fall:

Now to summarize from the Old and New Testament, the elect are the believers through out all the ages. In the Old Testament times, there were both Jews and Gentiles that were part of the elect but there were more Jews than Gentiles that were part of the elect. Also, in the New Testament times, there were both Gentiles and Jews that were part of the elect but there were more Gentiles than Jews that were part of the elect.

So, when God refers to humanity and the elect, God is referring to the believers whether they are Jews or Gentiles.

Chapter 14

Whosoever and the Great Commission
Whosoever means Everyone

There is something special about the word, "whosoever." Whosoever is a very inclusive word. Whosoever does mean anyone and everyone. When you put whosoever with the invitation to salvation for mankind, it means anyone and everyone is invited to be saved. With that said it also makes it clear that if we see the word, whosoever, in the Bible written with the invitation to be saved that God is inviting anyone and everyone to trust Christ as Savior. This could not occur if the individuals are already predetermined to heaven or hell.

Notice some of the passages in the Bible with the word, 'whosoever' in them. God invites all to be saved.

Joel 2:32 And it shall come to pass, *that* **whosoever shall call on the name of the LORD shall be delivered**: for in mount Zion and in Jerusalem shall be deliverance, as the LORD hath said, and in the remnant whom the LORD shall call.

Matthew 12:50 For **whosoever shall do the will of my Father which is in heaven,** the same is my brother, and sister, and mother.

Mark 3:35 For **whosoever** shall do the will of God, the same is my brother, and my sister, and mother.

Mark 10:15 Verily I say unto you, **Whosoever** shall not receive the kingdom of God as a little child, he shall not enter therein.

Luke 18:17 Verily I say unto you, **Whosoever** shall not receive the kingdom of God as a little child shall in no wise enter therein.

John 3:15 That **whosoever** believeth in him should not perish, but have eternal life.

John 3:16 For God so loved the world, that he gave his only begotten Son, that **whosoever** believeth in him should not perish, but have everlasting life.

John 4:14 But **whosoever** drinketh of the water that I shall give him shall never thirst; but the water that I shall give him shall be in him a well of water springing up into everlasting life.

John 11:26 And **whosoever** liveth and believeth in me shall never die. Believest thou this?

John 12:46 I am come a light into the world, that **whosoever** believeth on me should not abide in darkness.

Acts 2:21 And it shall come to pass, *that* **whosoever** <u>shall call on the name of the Lord shall be saved</u>.

Acts 10:43 To him give all the prophets witness, that through his name **whosoever** <u>believeth in him shall receive remission of sins.</u>

Romans 10:13 For **whosoever** <u>shall call upon the name of the Lord shall be saved.</u>

1 John 2:23 **Whosoever** <u>denieth the Son, the same hath not the Father</u>: *(but) he that acknowledgeth the Son hath the Father also.*

1 John 4:15 **Whosoever** <u>shall confess that Jesus is the Son of God, God dwelleth in him, and he in God</u>.

1 John 5:1 **Whosoever** <u>believeth that Jesus is the Christ is born of God</u>: and every one that loveth him that begat loveth him also that is begotten of him.

2 John 1:9 **Whosoever** <u>transgresseth, and abideth not in the doctrine of Christ, hath not God.</u> He that abideth in the doctrine of Christ, he hath both the Father and the Son.

Revelation 22:17 And the Spirit and the bride say, Come. And let him that heareth say, Come. And let him that is athirst come. And **whosoever** <u>will, let him take the water of life freely</u>.

The Great Commission is Universal

Matthew 28:19 Go ye therefore, and teach **all nations**, baptizing them in the name of the Father, and of the Son, and of the Holy Ghost: **20** Teaching them to observe all things whatsoever I have commanded you: and, lo, I am with you alway, *even* unto the end of the world. Amen.

Mark 16:15 And he said unto them, Go ye into **all the world**, and preach the gospel to **every creature.**

The Great Commission is very plain. The gospel is to be preached to every creature. So, if all are already predestined for Hell of Heaven as the Calvinist teaches, why bother giving them the gospel.

Chapter 15

An Explanation of Acts 13:48

Act 13:48 And when the Gentiles heard this, they were glad, and glorified the word of the Lord: and <u>as many as were **ordained** #*5021* to eternal life believed.</u>

> Notice the word study sentence below for the word, "ordained."

> "ordained" [G5021] tasso (8x) <u>addict</u>-1; <u>appoint</u>-3; <u>determine</u>-1; <u>ordain</u>-2; <u>set</u>-1

As many as were "ordained to eternal life" or "addicted to eternal life" or "determined to have eternal life" or "set their hearts on eternal life" believed. They were determined to have eternal life. They wanted eternal life. They believed in Jesus Christ for eternal life. If you want eternal life, if you are <u>determined</u> to have it, if your mind is <u>set</u> to possess eternal life you must believe in Jesus Christ as your Savior. This is the only way to get eternal life.

1 John 5:12 He that hath the Son hath life; *and* he that hath not the Son of God hath not life. **13** These things have I written unto you that believe on the name of the Son of God; that ye may know that ye have eternal life, and that ye may believe on the name of the Son of God.

John 6:68 Then Simon Peter answered him, Lord, to whom shall we go? <u>thou hast the words of eternal life.</u>

If you are determined to get eternal life, you must trust Jesus as your savior. Please study chapter 1 to make sure you are born again.

John 3:15 That whosoever believeth in him should not perish, but **have eternal life**.

John 3:16 For God so loved the world, that he gave his only begotten Son, that whosoever believeth in him should not perish, but **have everlasting life**.

John 3:18 He that believeth on him is not condemned: but he that believeth not is condemned already, because he hath not believed in the name of the only begotten Son of God.

John 3:36 He that believeth on the Son **hath everlasting life**: and he that believeth not the Son shall not see life; but the wrath of God abideth on him.

John 5:24 Verily, verily, I say unto you, He that heareth my word, and believeth on him that sent me, **hath everlasting life**, and shall not come into condemnation; but is passed from death unto life.

John 6:40 And this is the will of him that sent me, that every one which seeth the Son, and believeth on him,

may have everlasting life: and I will raise him up at the last day.

John 10:28 And **I give unto them eternal life**; and they shall never perish, neither shall any *man* pluck them out of my hand. **29** My Father, which gave *them* me, is greater than all; and no *man* is able to pluck *them* out of my Father's hand.

1 John 5:13 These things have I written unto you that believe on the name of the Son of God; that **ye may know that ye have eternal life**, and that ye may believe on the name of the Son of God.

Now notice the contrast in **Acts 13:46** Then Paul and Barnabas waxed bold, and said, It was necessary that the word of God should first have been spoken to you: but seeing ye put it from you, and **judge yourselves unworthy of everlasting life**, lo, we turn to the Gentiles.

They were unworthy of everlasting life because they refused to trust Christ as their Savior.

Warning: The word "ordained" (#5021 tasso) in Acts 13:48 is not the same Greek word as #4309 proorizo which is translated (ordain and predestine). Calvinists have attempted to make this verse say {*as many as were predestined to eternal life believed*}.

Chapter 16

An Explanation of Romans 8:15 - 33

An Explanation of Romans 8:15
We have received the Spirit of Adoption
and are waiting for the Adoption.

8:15 For ye have not received the spirit of bondage again to fear; but ye have received the Spirit of **adoption <5206>**, whereby we cry, Abba, Father.

> *Note: It says we have received the **SPIRIT of adoption** but not yet the adoption itself.*
>
> *Note: "adoption" [5206][5 times][Rom. 8:15, 23; 9:4; Gal. 4:5; Eph. 1:5]*
>
> *[All translated "adoption"][def. redemption of our body-Rom. 8:23]*
>
> *Note: "adoption" is future and is for the believer only. "waiting for adoption" Rom. 8:23*
>
> *It is predestinated for believers only and not for the unbelievers. Eph. 1:5*

8:16 The Spirit itself beareth witness with our spirit, that we are the children of God:

> *Note: The Holy Spirit of God uses the Word of God to assure us that upon trusting Christ as our Savior, we are*

the children of God. For an example see the following passage:

__I John__ __5:13__ These things have I written unto you that believe on the name of the Son of God; that ye may know that ye have eternal life, and that ye may believe on the name of the Son of God.

8:17 And if children, then heirs; heirs of God, and joint-heirs with Christ; if so be that we suffer with *him*, that we may be also glorified together.

8:18 For I reckon that **the sufferings of this present time** *are* not worthy *to be compared* with the glory which shall be revealed in us.

Note: The sufferings for the believer are grooming tools providentially given by God. They are designed by God to make us better. They should be considered extremely valuable.

__Rom__ __5:3__ And not only so, but we glory in tribulations also: knowing that tribulation worketh patience; __5:4__ And patience, experience; and experience, hope: __5:5__ And hope maketh not ashamed; because the love of God is shed abroad in our hearts by the Holy Ghost which is given unto us.

__1Pet__ __1:7__ That the trial of your faith, being much more precious than of gold

> *that perisheth, though it be tried with fire, might be found unto praise and honour and glory at the appearing of Jesus Christ:*

8:19 For the earnest expectation of the creature waiteth for the manifestation of the sons of God.

> *Note: **1John 3:1** Behold, what manner of love the Father hath bestowed upon us, that we should be called the sons of God: therefore the world knoweth us not, because it knew him not. **3:2** Beloved, **<u>now are we the sons of God</u>**, and it doth not yet appear what we shall be: but we know that, when he shall appear, we shall be like him; for we shall see him as he is.*

8:20 For the creature was made subject to vanity, not willingly, but by reason of him who hath subjected *the same* in hope,

8:21 Because the creature itself also shall be delivered from the bondage of corruption into the glorious liberty of the children of God.

8:22 For we know that the whole creation groaneth and travaileth in pain together until now.

An Explanation of Romans 8: 23

8:23 And not only [they], but ourselves also, which have the firstfruits of the Spirit, even we ourselves **groan**

<4727> within ourselves, waiting for the **adoption** **<5206>**, [to wit], the redemption of our body.

> *Note: "groan" [4727][6x][sighed-1; with grief-1; grudge-1; groan-3]*
>
> *Note: "adoption" [5206][5 times][see notes at v. 15]*

> *Note: Since the believer is waiting for the adoption, this means that the adoption even though promised has not yet occurred and it is future for the believer.*

8:24 For we are saved by hope: but hope that is seen is not hope: for what a man seeth, why doth he yet hope for?

8:25 But if we hope for that we see not, *then* do we with patience wait for *it*.

8:26 Likewise the Spirit also helpeth our infirmities: for we know not what we should pray for as we ought: but the Spirit itself maketh intercession for us with groanings which cannot be uttered.

> *Note: The Holy Spirit who has written the Word of God uses the Word of God to teach us how to pray.*

8:27 And he that searcheth the hearts knoweth what *is* the mind of the Spirit, because he maketh intercession for the saints according to *the will of* God.

8:28 And we know that all things work together for good to them that love God, to them who are the called according to *his* purpose.

An Explanation of Romans 8: 29-30

Foreknowledge and Predestination

8:29 For whom he did **foreknow** 4267, he also did **predestinate** 4309 [to be] conformed to the image of his Son, that he might be the firstborn among many brethren. **8:30** Moreover whom he did predestinate, them he also called: and whom he called, them he also justified: and whom he justified, them he also glorified.

> *Note: Predestination is based on God's foreknowledge just like election (1Pe 1:2) is based on God's foreknowledge. God looks down through time to see those who will believe and predestines those believers to their adoption, to their inheritance, and to conform them into the image of Christ. God looks down through time to see those who will believe and those believers are made part of God's elect.*

> *Note: "foreknow" [4267][5x][which knew from the beginning-Acts 26:5]*
> *[Rom. 8:29; 11:2-forknew; I Pet. 1:20-foreordained]*
> *[II Pet. 3:17-seeing ye know before]*

Note: "foreknowledge" [4268][2 times] [Acts 2:23; I Pet. 1:2]

Note: Foreknowledge is an attribute of God not an act of God. Just because God knows in advance what will happen does not make him responsible for what happens nor is it necessarily God's will on what happens in the future.

Example: Peter's denial: Matt. 26:34, 74; Mk. 14:30, 72; Lu. 22:34, 61; John 13:38. Jesus knew Peter was going to deny him, but it was not Jesus' fault or Jesus' will that Peter denied him. Study the following passages.

Matthew 26:34 *Jesus said unto him, Verily I say unto thee, **That this night, before the cock crow, thou shalt deny me thrice**.*

Matthew 26:74 *Then began he to curse and to swear, saying, I know not the man. And immediately the cock crew.*

Mark 14:30 *And Jesus saith unto him, Verily I say unto thee, **That this day, even in this night, before the cock crow twice, thou shalt deny me thrice**.*

Mark 14:72 *And the second time the cock crew. And Peter called to mind the word that Jesus said unto him, Before the cock crow twice, thou shalt deny me thrice. And when he thought thereon, he wept.*

Luke 22:34 *And he said, I tell thee, Peter**, the cock shall not crow this day, before that thou shalt thrice deny that thou knowest me**.*

Luke 22:61 *And the Lord turned, and looked upon Peter. And Peter remembered the word of the Lord, how he had said unto him, Before the cock crow, thou shalt deny me thrice.*

John 13:38 *Jesus answered him, Wilt thou lay down thy life for my sake? Verily, verily, I say unto thee, **The cock shall not crow, till thou hast denied me thrice**.*

*Note: "predestinate" [4309][6 times] [determined before-**Acts 4:28**; **Rom. 8:29**;*

***Rom. 8:30**; **I Cor. 2:7**-ordained; **Eph. 1:5, 11**]*

There are only five things mentioned in the Bible that are predestined by God. They are as follows:

1. *The crucifixion of our Lord:*
   Acts 4:26 *The kings of the earth stood up, and the rulers were gathered together against the Lord, and against his Christ.* **27** *For of a truth against thy holy child Jesus, whom thou hast anointed, both Herod, and Pontius Pilate, with the Gentiles, and the people of Israel, were gathered together,* **28** <u>**For to do whatsoever thy hand and thy counsel determined before to be done**</u>.

2. *The believer to be conformed into the image of Christ:*
   Romans 8:29 *For whom he did foreknow,* <u>***he also did predestinate to be conformed #4832 to the image of his Son***</u>, *that he might be the firstborn among many brethren.* **30** Moreover whom he did **predestinate** <4309>, them he also **called**: and whom he **called**, them he also **justified**: and whom he **justified**, them he also **glorified**.

   Because predestination is based on foreknowledge, it is put ahead of the calling. The calling is for salvation and is conditional. **(Matt. 20:16; 22:14)** *"Many are called, but few are chosen." The calling is complete when we answer the call by trusting Christ as our Savior. Upon answering the call by trusting Christ, we are justified. One day because of trusting Christ we will be glorified.*

Note: Note: "conformed" [#4832][2 times][Phil. 3:21-fashioned like unto]

3. *The wisdom of God written in God's Word:*
   1 Corinthians 2:7 *But we* <u>**speak the wisdom of God in a mystery, even the hidden wisdom, which God ordained before the world unto our glory**</u>*:*

4. *The believer's adoption:*
   Ephesians 1:5 *Having predestinated us unto the adoption of children by Jesus Christ to himself, according to the good pleasure of his will,*

5. *The believer's inheritance:*
   Ephesians 1:11 *In whom also* <u>**we have obtained an inheritance, being predestinated**</u> *according to the purpose*

of him who worketh all things after the counsel of his own will:

8:31 What shall we then say to these things? If God *be* for us, who *can be* against us?

8:32 He that spared not his own Son, but delivered him up for us all, how shall he not with him also freely give us all things?

An Explanation of Romans 8:33

No One can Condemn When God Justifies

8:33 Who shall lay any thing to the charge of God's **elect #1588**? [It is] God that justifieth.

> *Note: "elect" [1588][23 times][chosen-7; elect-13; elect's-3]*
>
> *Note: "election" [1589][7 times] [chosen-1 ; election-6]*
>
> *Remember election shuts no one out but a lot of people in.*

> *2 Thessalonians 2:13 But we are bound to give thanks alway to God for you, brethren beloved of the Lord, because God hath from the beginning chosen you to salvation through sanctification of the Spirit and belief of the truth:*

Belief of the truth is the condition of election. There is no such thing as "unconditional election".

1 Peter 1:2 <u>Elect according to the foreknowledge of God the Father</u>, *through sanctification of the Spirit, unto obedience and sprinkling of the blood of Jesus Christ: Grace unto you, and peace, be multiplied.*

(I Peter 1:2) says election is according to God's foreknowledge. God has chosen us from the past because he knows we will choose him in the future.

Chapter 17

An Explanation of Romans 9:11-24

God's Purpose and God's Will

9:11 (For [the children] being not yet born, neither having done any good or evil, that the **purpose #4286** of God according to **election #1589** might stand, not of works, but of him that calleth;)

> *Note: Remember election is based on foreknowledge. (1Peter 1:2) God calls us not based on our works but based on us trusting Christ as our Savior and His foreknowledge. He looks down through time to see if we are going to trust Christ as our Savior. Knowing that we will trust Christ makes us part of the elect.*

> *Note: "purpose" [4286][12x] [shewbread-4; purpose-8]*

> *Note: "election" [1589][7x][chosen; election-6]*

> *Note: Just like God's will is for all to be saved. [**II Pet. 3:9; I Tim. 2:4; 4:10**]*
> *God also has a purpose for everyone. This purpose is according to election*

or our choosing God as well as God choosing us.

Note: Election is conditional. See **II Thess. 2:13** *"God hath from the beginning chosen you to salvation <u>through</u> sanctification of the Spirit and* **belief of the truth**.*"*
Election shuts no one out but a lot of people in.

9:12 It was said unto her, The elder shall serve the younger.
Note: C.R. Gen. 25:23 This is an example of God's foreknowledge. Remember foreknowledge is an attribute of God. It is not an act of God. God knowing something will happen does not mean that it is God's will that it happens.

9:13 As it is written, Jacob have I loved, but Esau have I **hated**. *(Loved less)*
Note: C.R. **Malachi 1:2** *I have loved you, saith the LORD. Yet ye say, Wherein hast thou loved us? Was not Esau Jacob's brother? saith the LORD: <u>yet I loved Jacob</u>, 3 And <u>I **hated** Esau,</u> and laid his mountains and his heritage waste for the dragons of the wilderness.*

> *Note: An example of hate found in* **Luke 14:26** *"and **hate** not his father, and mother,"* **Hate** *in Romans 9:13 is the same Greek word as **hate** in* **Luke 14:26**. *Hate is defined in* **Mat.10:37** *as 'not loving more' or 'loving less'.*
>
> **Matt 10:37** *He that **loveth** father or mother **more** than me is not worthy of me: and he that **loveth** son or daughter **more** than me is not worthy of me.*
>
> *The passage in Mal. 1:2-3 is also dealing with the nation of Israel and the nation of Esau and not Jacob and Esau as individuals.*

9:14 What shall we say then? [Is there] unrighteousness with God? God forbid.

The Mercy of God upon All

9:15 For he saith to Moses, I will have mercy on whom I will have mercy, and I will have compassion on whom I will have compassion.

> *Note: C.R.* **Ex. 33:19** *And he said, I will make all my goodness pass before thee, and I will proclaim the name of the LORD before thee; <u>and will be gracious to whom I will be gracious, and will shew mercy on whom I will shew mercy.</u>*

*Note: **Rom. 11:32** says "For God hath concluded them all in unbelief, **that he might have mercy upon all**." Rom. 9:15 does not say God will condemn who He will condemn. It says, "He will have mercy on whom He will have mercy."*

9:16 So then [it is] not of him that willeth, nor of him that runneth, but of God that sheweth mercy.

Note: This is why salvation is by grace. See the following passages.

*   **Eph 2:5** Even when we were dead in sins, hath quickened us together with Christ, (**by grace ye are saved**;)*

*   **Eph 2:8** For **by grace are ye saved through faith**; and that not of yourselves: it is the gift of God: **2:9** Not of works, lest any man should boast.*

*   **Rom 3:24 Being justified freely by his grace** through the redemption that is in Christ Jesus:*

We do not go to heaven because we simply want to or because of any deed we do. We go to heaven because of what Jesus did for us on the cross and us appealing to God's mercy and asking Jesus to save our souls. See the following passage.

> *Luke 18:13 And the publican, standing afar off, would not lift up so much as his eyes unto heaven, but smote upon his breast, saying, <u>God be merciful to me a sinner</u>.*

The Purpose of God for Pharaoh

9:17 For the scripture saith unto Pharaoh, Even for this same purpose have I raised thee up, that I might shew my power in thee, and that my name might be declared throughout all the earth.

> *Note: C.R. **Exodus 9:16** And in very deed for this cause have I raised thee up, for to shew in thee my power; and that my name may be declared throughout all the earth.*

> *Note: If God showed His power in and through Pharaoh as a lost man, imagine what God would have done in and through him as a saved man.*

9:18 Therefore hath he mercy on whom he will [have mercy], and whom he will he hardeneth.

> *Note: God hardened Pharaoh's heart to not let the children of Israel go. Before God did this Pharaoh had already hardened his own heart in rejecting the great Salvation. Notice the following passage.*

> **Exod 5:2** *And Pharaoh said, <u>**Who is the LORD, that I should obey his voice to let Israel go? I know not the LORD, neither will I let Israel go.**</u>*

Resisting God's Will

9:19 Thou wilt say then unto me, Why doth he yet find fault? For <u>who hath **resisted <436>** his **will <1013>**</u>?

> *Note: "resisted" [436][14 times] [withstand-5; resist-9]*

> *Note: "will" [1013][2 times][will; purpose]*

> *Note: Many have resisted God's will. (Example) the children of Israel:*

> **Acts 7:51** *Ye stiffnecked and uncircumcised in heart and ears, <u>ye do always resist the Holy Ghost: as your fathers did, so do ye.</u>*

> *Note: This verse is not teaching that God's will cannot be resisted or that there is such a thing as irresistible grace. The point is <u>who has resisted God's will and prospered</u>? No one has. There is no such thing as irresistible grace. Notice the following passage.*

Job 9:4 *He is wise in heart, and mighty in strength:* **<u>who hath hardened himself against him, and hath prospered?</u>**

Replying against God's Purpose

9:20 Nay but, O man, who art thou that repliest against God? Shall the thing formed say to him that formed [it], Why hast thou made me thus?

The Potter Has Power over the Clay Vessels unto Honor and Vessels unto Dishonor and Wrath

9:21 Hath not the potter power over the clay, of the same lump to make <u>one vessel unto honour, and another unto dishonour?</u>

> *Note: It does not say, (make vessels **of** honor or **of** dishonor) It says to make vessels **unto** honor and **unto** dishonor. To receive Jesus Christ as Savior makes you a vessel of honor. If a person chooses to reject Christ, he is a vessel of dishonor. In spite of unbelief, God will use the vessel of dishonor in some ways as God sees fit.*

> *Note: "honour" [5092][45x][honour-35; precious-1; price-8; sum-1]*

Note: "dishonour" [819][7x] [dishonour-4; reproach-1; shame-1; vile-1]

Vessels of Wrath

9:22 [What] if God, willing to shew [his] wrath, and to make his power known, endured with much **longsuffering #3115** the vessels of wrath **fitted #2675** to **destruction #684**:

Note: "longsuffering" [3115][14 times] [longsuffering-12; patience-2]

Note: "fitted" [2675][13x][mend-2; perfect-6; perfectly joined together; prepared; framed; restore; fitted]

Note: "destruction" [684][20x][waste-2; perdition-8; die-1; damnable-1; perish-1; pernicious-1; destruction-5]

Note: God shows much patience and longsuffering toward the vessels of wrath but so many still refuse the Great Salvation God offers to all. Rejecting Christ as Savior makes you a vessel that is fit to destruction.

Vessels of Mercy

9:23 And that he might make known the riches of his glory on the **vessels of mercy**, which he had **afore #4282 prepared #4282** unto glory,

Note: "afore prepared" [4282][2x][Eph. 2:10-hath before ordained]

proetoinazo {pro 4253 before}{hetoinazo 2090 to make ready}

Note: The preparation took place on the vessels of mercy or on the believers in the past due to foreknowledge knowing that the vessels of mercy would trust Christ as their Savior

9:24 Even us, whom he hath called, not of the Jews only, but also of the Gentiles?

Note: Because of answering the call of Salvation, we are vessels of mercy whether we be Jew or Gentile.

Chapter 18

An Explanation of John 12:37-40

John 12:37 But though he had done so many miracles before them, <u>yet they</u> **believed not** <u>on him:</u>
> *Note: Before the Jews refused to believe the miracles that Jesus did, they refused to believe the salvation that Jesus offered.*

John 12:38 That the saying of Esaias the prophet might be fulfilled, which he spake, Lord, who hath believed our report? and to whom hath the arm of the Lord been revealed?
> *Note: C.R.* **Isa 53:1** *Who hath believed our report? and to whom is the arm of the LORD revealed?*

John 12:39 Therefore **they could not believe**, because that Esaias said again,
John 12:40 He hath blinded their eyes, and hardened their heart; that they should not see with *their* eyes, nor understand with *their* heart, and be converted, and I should heal them.
> *Note: C.R.* **Isa 6:10** *Make the heart of this people fat, and make their ears heavy, and shut their eyes; lest they see with their eyes, and hear with their ears,*

and understand with their heart, and convert, and be healed.

Note: God blinds their eyes and hardens their heart because they believed not the record of God's word. Notice: **Romans 10:17** *"So then faith cometh by hearing, and hearing by the word of God." So, if a person refuses to believe the Bible and the gospel, God will blind them from believing even the miracles they witnessed. It is a dangerous thing to not believe the Bible. This is in no wise an encroachment on the free will of man. Man chooses to reject the gospel and not believe the Bible and because of it, God blinds them in more unbelief. So, it is unbelief on their part that brings more blindness on them from God.*

Notice: **2Co 4:4** *In whom* **the god of this world hath** **blinded the minds of them** **which believe not,** *lest the light of the glorious gospel of Christ, who is the image of God, should shine unto them.*

Also **Romans 11:20** *Well;* **because of** **unbelief** *they were broken off, and thou standest by faith. Be not highminded, but fear:*

A Calvinist wants, really bad, to say that God blinded them so they could not be saved. This is not true. It is because of their unbelief they could not be saved. Notice the following passages.

John 3:18 He that believeth on him is not condemned: **but he that believeth not is condemned already, because he hath not believed in the name of the only begotten Son of God.**

John 3:36 He that believeth on the Son hath everlasting life: and **he that believeth not the Son shall not see life; but the wrath of God abideth on him.**

Chapter 19

An Explanation of Jude 4

Jud 1:4 For there are certain men crept in unawares, <u>who were **before of old ordained to this condemnation**</u>, ungodly men, turning the grace of our God into lasciviousness, and **denying the only Lord God, and our Lord Jesus Christ.**

Note: "before ordained" #4270 (5x) (write-1; write aforetime-1; write afore-1; evidently set forth-1; before ordained-1 [Def. written before]

Note: So, to insert the definition in place: 'certain men who were written before to this condemnation, ungodly men'.

*Note: There are countless examples of ungodly men and their condemnation written in the Old Testament and previously written in the New Testament. Note: "ordained" here does not mean predestined. The reason for their condemnation is stated in the latter part of the verse. "**Denying the only Lord God, and our Lord Jesus Christ.**"*

Chapter 20

The Divine Order

In the following passages there is a divine order given of which things that God acts with the attribute that God has from the first down to the last. God has first 1) foreknowledge, and then God's actions are as follows. 2) predestination, 3) calling; 4) justification, and finally 5) glorification.

Romans 8:29 For whom he did **foreknow**, he also did **predestinate** *to be* conformed to the image of his Son, that he might be the firstborn among many brethren. **30** Moreover whom he did **predestinate**, them he also **called**: and whom he **called**, them he also **justified**: and whom he **justified**, them he also **glorified**.

From the passage above we can see God's divine order of these five major actions or attributes that are performed by God Himself on the behalf of a person that has trusted Christ as Savior. The summary of all the actions and attributes are as follows. **Foreknowledge** comes **first** because by it, God looks through time and knows everything that will ever happen either good or bad before it even happens. **Predestination** is **second** in order which by foreknowledge locks in the five issues mentioned in the Bible in which three apply to believers. All five are discussed in this book. The **call** is the **third** in the order which is a universal call which states that whosoever shall call upon the name of the Lord shall be saved. The **fourth** is when the call is answered by the individual, the individual is immediately and permanently **justified**. The **fifth** is one day at the end of the believer's life, that believer will be **glorified**. The explanation of each action and attribute is listed in order and explained below.

1) Foreknowledge:

Remember just because God knows something will happen ahead of time, does not make God responsible for it or even for it to be God's will for that to happen. Foreknowledge is an attribute of God not an act of God. God looks into the future to see who will trust Christ as their Savior and who will not trust Christ.

2) Predestination:

Remember predestination is based on the foreknowledge of God. As has already been discussed, there are only five things mentioned in the Bible that are predestined. What is mentioned here in the **Romans 8:29** is the believer to be conformed into the image of Christ. Because of God's foreknowledge, God is able to see into the future and see who will trust Christ as their personal Savior. Those that do are predestined to be conformed into the image of Christ.

3) Calling:

This calling works together with God choosing us. This calling goes together with election. This calling refers not only to God's invitation to get saved but also man's response by trusting Christ as Savior to be saved.

> **Revelation 17:14** These shall make war with the Lamb, and the Lamb shall overcome them: for he is Lord of lords, and King of kings: and they that are with him *are* **called, and chosen, and faithful.**

> **1 Peter 2:9** But ye *are* a **chosen** generation, a royal priesthood, an holy nation, a peculiar people; that ye should shew forth the praises of him who hath **called** you out of darkness into his marvellous light:

4) Justification:

The moment a person trusts Christ as Savior he is justified. Notice the following verses.

> **Acts 13:39** And by him **all that believe are justified from all things**, from which ye could not be justified by the law of Moses.

Romans 3:20 Therefore by the deeds of the law there shall no flesh be justified in his sight: for by the law *is* the knowledge of sin.

Romans 3:24 <u>Being justified freely by his grace through the redemption that is in Christ Jesus:</u>

Romans 3:26 To declare, *I say*, at this time his righteousness: that **<u>he might be just, and the justifier of him which believeth in Jesus.</u>**

Romans 3:28 Therefore we conclude that **<u>a man is justified by faith without the deeds of the law.</u>**

Romans 3:30 Seeing *it is* one God, which shall justify the circumcision by faith, and uncircumcision through faith.

Romans 4:2 For if Abraham were justified by works, he hath *whereof* to glory; but not before God.

Romans 4:5 But to him that worketh not, but believeth on him that justifieth the ungodly, his faith is counted for righteousness.

Romans 5:1 Therefore **being justified by faith**, we have peace with God through our Lord Jesus Christ:

Romans 5:9 Much more then, being now justified by his blood, we shall be saved from wrath through him.

Galatians 2:16 Knowing that **a man is not justified by the works of the law, but by the faith of Jesus Christ**, even we have believed in Jesus Christ, that we might be justified by the faith of Christ, and not by the works of the law: for by the works of the law shall no flesh be justified.

Galatians 3:8 And the scripture, foreseeing that **God would justify the heathen through faith**, preached before the gospel unto Abraham, *saying*, In thee shall all nations be blessed.

Galatians 3:11 But that no man is justified by the law in the sight of God, *it is* evident: for, The just shall live by faith.

Galatians 3:24 Wherefore the law was our schoolmaster *to bring us* unto

Christ, that **we might be justified by faith.**

5) Glorification:

One day every believer will be glorified for eternity. At this point is when the believer receives a glorified body. This is also called in the scripture, the believer's **adoption.** It according to **Rom. 8:23** is the final stage of our redemption. Notice the following verses.

Romans 8:18 For I reckon that the sufferings of this present time *are* not worthy *to be compared* with **the glory which shall be revealed in us.**

1 Corinthians 15:44 It is sown a natural body; it is raised a **spiritual body**. There is a natural body, and there is a **spiritual body**.

1 Corinthians 15:53 For this corruptible must put on **incorruption**, and this mortal *must* put on **immortality**. **54** So when this corruptible shall have put on **incorruption**, and this mortal shall have put on **immortality**, then shall be brought to pass the saying that is written, Death is swallowed up in victory.

2 Corinthians 5:1 For we know that if our earthly house of *this* tabernacle were dissolved, **we have a building of God, an house not made with hands, eternal in the heavens**.

Romans 8:23 And not only *they*, but ourselves also, which have the firstfruits of the Spirit, even we ourselves groan within ourselves, waiting for **the adoption, *to wit*, the redemption of our body.**

1 Peter 5:1 The elders which are among you I exhort, who am also an elder, and a witness of the sufferings of Christ, and also **a partaker of the glory that shall be revealed**:

Chapter 21

Was Pharaoh King of Egypt Predestined for Hell?

One of the examples that the Calvinists seem to want to bring up is the Pharaoh of Egypt in Moses' day. God is said to harden Pharaoh's heart. So, the question is, "Did God harden Pharaoh's heart about getting saved so that Pharaoh could not get saved?" Was Pharaoh predestined to Hell?

Notice what Paul says in the book of Romans about Pharaoh. God makes it very clear that Pharaoh was hardened by God to glorify His name through the mighty deeds that He displayed in Egypt to show his might throughout all the world. Pharaoh hardened his own heart concerning the salvation of his soul. Notice the following passage.

Exod 5:2 And Pharaoh said, **Who _is_ the LORD, that I should obey his voice to let Israel go? I know not the LORD**, neither will I let Israel go.

Rom 9:17 For the scripture saith unto Pharaoh, **Even for this same purpose have I raised thee up, that I might shew my power in thee, and that my name might be declared throughout all the earth. 9:18** Therefore hath he mercy on whom he will _have mercy_, and whom he will he hardeneth.

Allow me to address the statement in verse 18,

"hath he mercy on whom he will have mercy." Notice the following passage. **Rom 11:32** For God hath concluded them all in unbelief, **that he might have mercy upon all**.

This quotation from Rom. 9:17 comes from Ex. 9:16 written below.

Ex 9:16 And in very deed for this *cause* have I raised thee up, for to shew *in* thee my power; and that my name may be declared throughout all the earth.

Let us take a closer look at the verses in Exodus about God hardening Pharaoh's heart.

Exod 4:21 And the LORD said unto Moses, When thou goest to return into Egypt, see that thou do all those wonders before Pharaoh, which I have put in thine hand: **but I will harden his heart, that he shall not let the people go.**

Exod 7:3 And **I will harden Pharaoh's heart**, and multiply my signs and my wonders in the land of Egypt.

Exod 7:13 And **he hardened Pharaoh's heart, that he hearkened not unto them**; as the LORD had said.

Exod 7:14 And the LORD said unto Moses, **Pharaoh's heart [is] hardened, he refuseth to let the people go.**

Exod 7:22 And the magicians of Egypt did so with their enchantments: and **Pharaoh's heart was hardened, neither did he hearken unto them; as the LORD had said**.

Exod 8:15 But when Pharaoh saw that there was respite, **he hardened his heart, and hearkened not unto them; as the LORD had said.**

Exod 8:19 Then the magicians said unto Pharaoh, This [is] the finger of God: and **Pharaoh's heart was hardened**, and he hearkened not unto them; as the LORD had said.

Exod 8:32 And **Pharaoh hardened his heart** at this time also, neither would he let the people go.

Exod 9:7 And Pharaoh sent, and, behold, there was not one of the cattle of the Israelites dead. And **the heart of Pharaoh was hardened, and he did not let the people go**.

Exod 9:12 And **the LORD hardened the heart of Pharaoh**, and he hearkened not unto them; as the LORD had spoken unto Moses.

Exod 9:34 And when Pharaoh saw that the rain and the hail and the thunders were ceased, he sinned yet more, and **hardened his heart**, he and his servants.

Exod 9:35 And **the heart of Pharaoh was hardened, neither would he let the children of Israel go; as the LORD had spoken** by Moses.

Exod 10:1 And the LORD said unto Moses, Go in unto Pharaoh: for **I have hardened his heart**, and the heart of his servants, that I might shew these my signs before him:

Exod 10:20 But t**he LORD hardened Pharaoh's heart, so that he would not let the children of Israel go**.

Exod 10:27 But **the LORD hardened Pharaoh's heart, and he would not let them go.**

Exod 11:10 And Moses and Aaron did all these wonders before Pharaoh: and **the LORD hardened Pharaoh's heart, so that he would not let the children of Israel go** out of his land.

Exod 14:4 And **I will harden Pharaoh's heart**, that he shall follow after them; and I will be honoured upon Pharaoh, and upon all his host; that the Egyptians may know that I [am] the LORD. And they did so.

Exod 14:8 And **the LORD hardened the heart of Pharaoh king of Egypt**, and he pursued after the children of Israel: and the children of Israel went out with an high hand.

You will notice in every case in the verses above it is stated that God hardens Pharaoh's heart about letting the children of Israel go and nothing is said about God hardening Pharaoh's heart concerning the salvation of his soul. It is worth repeating that Pharaoh hardened his own heart about the matter of getting saved before God hardened Pharaoh's heart about letting the children of Israel go. Notice again the following passage.

Exod 5:2 And Pharaoh said, **Who is the LORD, that I should obey his voice to let Israel go? I know not the LORD**, neither will I let Israel go.

Chapter 22

Was Jeremiah and John the Baptist Predestined for Heaven Before they Got Saved?

Notice the following passages concerning Jeremiah and John the Baptist, who have been brought up by Calvinists to suggest that these men were predestined for heaven before they got saved.

Jeremiah
Jer 1:5 Before I formed thee in the belly I knew thee; and before thou camest forth out of the womb I sanctified thee, *and* I ordained thee a prophet unto the nations.

John the Baptist
Luke 1:41 And it came to pass, that, when Elisabeth heard the salutation of Mary, **the babe leaped in her womb**; and Elisabeth was filled with the Holy Ghost:

Luke 1:15 For he shall be great in the sight of the Lord, and shall drink neither wine nor strong drink; and **he shall be filled with the Holy Ghost, even from his mother's womb**.

Because of God's foreknowledge, God can look down through time at Jeremiah and see past his birth and his second birth and on into his ministry. This in no wise suggests that Jeremiah did not need to get saved. When he got old enough like anyone else, he was born again.

John the Baptist, while in his mother's womb, responded physically and noticeably by his mother, and leaped in her womb when hearing the voice of Mary. As said before, this in no wise suggests that John the Baptist was already saved and did not need when old enough to be born again like everyone else in order to go to heaven. The fact that John the Baptist was filled with the Holy Spirit while in his mother's womb still does not imply that John the Baptist was already saved or did not need to get saved. In the womb, John the Baptist was neither lost nor was he already saved. John the Baptist like any other unborn child or even born child was safely below the age of accountability. When the child grows old enough and becomes able to understand that he is a sinner and sees his responsibility to get saved; then John must be saved like anyone else and like he himself preached. So, everyone must be born again when getting to the age of accountability and there are no exceptions.

Notice the following passage of scripture that is a quote of John the Baptist' preaching on salvation.

John 3:27 <u>John answered and said</u>, A man can receive nothing, except it be given him from heaven. **3:28** Ye yourselves bear me witness, that I said, I am not the Christ, but that I am sent before him. **3:29** He that hath the bride is the bridegroom: but the friend of the bridegroom, which standeth and heareth him, rejoiceth greatly because of the bridegroom's voice: this my joy therefore is fulfilled. **3:30** He must increase, but I *must* decrease. **3:31** He that cometh from above is above all: he that is of the earth is earthly, and speaketh of the earth: he that cometh from heaven is above all. **3:32** And what he hath seen and heard, that he testifieth; and no man receiveth his testimony. **3:33** He that hath received his testimony hath set to his seal that God is true. **3:34** For he whom God hath sent speaketh the words of God: for God giveth not the Spirit by measure *unto him*. **3:35** The Father loveth the Son, and hath given all things into his hand. **3:36** <u>**He that believeth on the Son hath everlasting life: and he that believeth not the Son shall not see life; but the wrath of God abideth on him**</u>.

From the previous passage, we can be sure that John the Baptist believed and practiced what he himself preached. John the Baptist when getting old enough trusted Christ as Savior like anyone else who is born again.

Chapter 23

The Calvinist Must Believe that God Never Changes His Mind

If a person is going to believe as the Calvinist does, that everything is predetermined and every action is set in stone, he will have to believe that God never changes His mind. The Calvinist will go on about God being All-Knowing and All-Powerful which of course is true but we must realize that God allows for man to have choices and gives room for man to see the results of his choices, good or bad, so that man will learn from his choices and be punished or rewarded accordingly. The problem with believing that God never changes His mind is that the Bible tells us in several instances that God indeed changed His mind. It was not because of a flaw in God's thinking. It was because of the action and reaction of man to sin and sinful situations. God simply is accordingly responding to man's actions. Notice the following example about the design of Hell itself.

Matt 25:41 Then shall he say also unto them on the left hand, **Depart from me, ye cursed, into everlasting fire, prepared for the devil and his angels:**

Notice from this passage above that Hell or Everlasting Fire was originally designed for the devil and his angels. Because of the wickedness of man rejecting the Christ as his Savior, the purpose and intent of the design was altered somewhat to accommodate humans as well. So, we see that God changed his mind to accommodate humans going to Hell as well as the Devil and his fallen Angels.

2Thess 1:7 And to you who are troubled rest with us, when the Lord Jesus shall be revealed from heaven with his mighty angels,

2Thess 1:8 <u>In flaming fire taking vengeance on them that know not God, and that obey not the gospel of our Lord Jesus Christ:</u>

2Thess 1:9 <u>Who shall be punished with everlasting destruction from the presence of the Lord, and from the glory of his power;</u>

In the following passages we will show the reader many times where God changed His mind to accommodate for the wicked choices of mankind.

Gen 6:6 And **<u>it repented the LORD that he had made man</u>** on the earth, and it grieved him at his heart.

Gen 6:7 And the LORD said, I will destroy man whom I have created from the face of the earth; both man, and beast, and the creeping thing, and the fowls of the air; **<u>for it repenteth me that I have made them.</u>**

From the passage above we see that God repented or changed His mind about the very creation of man himself. As a side note, this flies in the face of the individuals out there that are teaching that repent means to turn from sin. Since God cannot sin, God does not turn from sin. Repent is to have a genuine change of mind. Please see this author's book on "How to Study the Bible for Yourself" and "Repentance."

Now notice other places in the Bible where God repented or changed His mind. In the following passages, God changes His mind about the judgement he would bring on his people, depending on how they respond to God's will.

Exod 32:12 Wherefore should the Egyptians speak, and say, For mischief did he bring them out, to slay them in the mountains, and to consume them from the face of the earth? **Turn from thy fierce wrath, and repent of this evil against thy people**.

Exod 32:14 And **the LORD repented of the evil which he thought to do unto his people**.

Judg 2:18 And when the LORD raised them up judges, then the LORD was with the judge, and delivered them out of the hand of their enemies all the days of the judge: for **it repented the LORD because of their groanings by reason of them that oppressed them and vexed them**.

In the next passages, God changes His mind about making Saul king because of Saul's wickedness.

1Sam 15:11 <u>**It repenteth me that I have set up Saul** *to* *be* **king**</u>: for he is turned back from following me, and hath not performed my commandments. And it grieved Samuel; and he cried unto the LORD all night.

1Sam 15:35 And Samuel came no more to see Saul until the day of his death: nevertheless Samuel mourned for Saul: and <u>**the LORD repented that he had made Saul king over Israel**</u>.

Now notice more places in the Bible where God repented or changed His mind. In the following passages, God changes His mind about the judgement he would bring on His people, depending on how they respond to God's will or even the good that He will do to His people.

2Sam 24:16 And when the angel stretched out his hand upon Jerusalem to destroy it, <u>**the LORD repented him of the evil**</u>, and said to the angel that destroyed the people, It is enough: stay now thine hand. And the angel of the LORD was by the threshingplace of Araunah the Jebusite.

1Chr 21:15 And God sent an angel unto Jerusalem to destroy it: and as he was destroying, the LORD beheld, and <u>**he repented him of the evil**</u>, and said to the angel that destroyed, It is enough, stay now thine hand. And the angel of the LORD stood by the threshingfloor of Ornan the Jebusite.

Ps 106:45 And he remembered for them his covenant, and **repented according to the multitude of his mercies.**

Ps 135:14 For the LORD will judge his people, and **he will repent himself concerning his servants.**

Jer 18:8 If that nation, against whom I have pronounced, turn from their evil, **I will repent of the evil that I thought to do unto them.**

Jer 18:10 **If it do evil in my sight, that it obey not my voice, then I will repent of the good, wherewith I said I would benefit them.**

Jer 26:13 Therefore now **amend your ways and your doings, and obey the voice of the LORD your God; and the LORD will repent him of the evil that he hath pronounced against you.**

Jer 26:19 Did Hezekiah king of Judah and all Judah put him at all to death? did he not fear the LORD, and besought the LORD, and **the LORD repented him of the evil which he had pronounced against them**? Thus might we procure great evil against our souls.

Jer 42:10 If ye will still abide in this land, then will I build you, and not pull *you* down, and I will plant you, and not pluck *you* up: for **I repent me of the evil that I have done unto you**.

Joel 2:13 And rend your heart, and not your garments, and turn unto the LORD your God: for **he *is* gracious and merciful, slow to anger, and of great kindness, and repenteth him of the evil**.

Joel 2:14 Who knoweth *if* he will return and repent, and leave a blessing behind him; *even* a meat offering and a drink offering unto the LORD your God?

Jonah 3:9 Who can tell *if* **God will turn and repent**, and turn away from his fierce anger, that we perish not? **Jonah 3:10** And God saw their works, that they turned from their evil way; and **God repented of the evil, that he had said that he would do unto them; and he did *it* not.**

We will also notice that God changes ways in the Bible concerning the affairs of mankind. Notice the following things that God has changed through the years.

1) Sabbath Days were changed and fulfilled:
    A. The Sabbath days nailed to the cross:
        Col. 2:14 Blotting out the handwriting of ordinances that was against us, which was contrary to us, and took it out of the way, nailing it to his cross; **2:15** And having spoiled principalities and powers, he made a shew of them openly, triumphing over them in it. **2:16** Let no

man therefore judge you in meat, or in drink, or in respect of an holyday, or of the new moon, or of the sabbath days:

B. The Sabbath days were between Israel and God

Ex. 31:13 Speak thou also unto the children of Israel, saying, Verily my Sabbaths ye shall keep: for it is a sign between me and you throughout your generations;

Ex. 31:17 It is a sign between me and the children of Israel for ever: for in six days the Lord made heaven and earth, and on the seventh day he rested, and was refreshed.

C. The First Day of the Week

1 Corinthians 16:2 <u>Upon the first *day* of the week</u> let every one of you lay by him in store, as *God* hath prospered him, that there be no gatherings when I come.

Acts 20:7 And upon **<u>the first *day* of the week</u>**, when the disciples came together to break bread, Paul preached unto them, ready to depart on the morrow; and continued his speech until midnight.

2) Dietary Laws of Leviticus Chapter 11 are no longer in effect.

Acts 10:11 And saw heaven opened, and a certain vessel descending unto him, as it had been a great sheet knit at the four corners, and let down to the earth: **10:12 <u>Wherein were all manner of fourfooted beasts of the earth, and wild beasts, and creeping things, and fowls of the air.</u> 10:13** And there came a voice to him, Rise, Peter; kill, and eat. **10:14** But Peter said, Not so, Lord; for I have never eaten any thing that is common or unclean. **10:15** And the voice *spake* unto him again the second time, **<u>What God hath cleansed, *that* call not thou common.</u>**

1Tim 4:1 Now the Spirit speaketh expressly, that in the latter times some shall depart from the faith, giving heed to seducing spirits, and doctrines of devils; **4:2** Speaking lies in hypocrisy; having their conscience seared with a hot iron; **4:3** Forbidding to marry, and **<u>commanding to abstain from meats</u>, <u>which God hath created to be received with thanksgiving</u>** of them which believe and know the truth. **4:4** For every creature of God is good, and nothing to be refused, if it be received with thanksgiving:

Col. 2:14 Blotting out the handwriting of ordinances that was against us, which was contrary to us, and took it out of the way, nailing it to his cross; **2:15** And having spoiled principalities and powers, he made a shew of them openly, triumphing over them in it. **2:16 Let no man therefore judge you in meat**, or **in drink**, or in respect of an holyday, or of the new moon, or of the sabbath days:"

3) Circumcision is no longer in effect:

Gal 5:6 For in Jesus Christ neither circumcision availeth any thing, nor uncircumcision; but faith which worketh by love.

Gal 6:15 For in Christ Jesus neither circumcision availeth any thing, nor uncircumcision, but a new creature.

1Cor 7:18 Is any man called being circumcised? let him not become uncircumcised. Is any called in uncircumcision? let him not be circumcised. **7:19** Circumcision is nothing, and uncircumcision is nothing, but the keeping of the commandments of God.

4) Animal sacrifices are no longer practiced:

Heb 9:12 Neither by the blood of goats and calves, but by his own blood he entered in once into the holy place, having obtained eternal redemption *for us.*

Heb 7:27 Who needeth not daily, as those high priests, to offer up sacrifice, first for his own sins, and then for the people's: for this he did once, when he offered up himself.

Heb 10:10 By the which will we are sanctified through the offering of the body of Jesus Christ once *for all.*

It is also important to point out that God will never repent or change His mind about a promise He has made. See the following passages.

Num 23:19 <u>God *is* not a man, that he should lie; neither the son of man, that he should repent: hath he said, and shall he not do *it*? or hath he spoken, and shall he not make it good</u>?

Ezek 24:14 <u>I the LORD have spoken *it*: it shall come to pass, and I will do *it*; I will not go back, neither will I spare, neither will I repent</u>; according to thy ways, and according to thy doings, shall they judge thee, saith the Lord GOD.

So, in concluding this chapter, if everything is predestined, God would never need to change His mind concerning the affairs of mankind. We have seen from the Bible that God changed His mind about creating man, about making Saul king, and about the judgment on people and even about the good He would do for people. God has also changed dietary laws, sacrificial laws, sabbath days, and circumcision. However, God will never change His mind about a Promise He makes. God will never break any promise that He has made. With this in mind, allow me to leave this chapter with one of God's special promises.

1John 2:25 <u>And this is the promise that he hath promised us, *even* eternal life.</u>

Chapter 24

<u>What is Meant by the Word, "Sovereign?"</u>

One of the words that might come up when studying Calvinism is the word, sovereign. The reader might be surprised because this word is not in the Bible. Please do not be alarmed, the word, "Trinity," does not appear in the Bible either but the definition of the word, Trinity, does appear in the Bible. It is in **I John 5:7.**

1John 5:7 For there are three that bear record in heaven, the Father, the Word, and the Holy Ghost: and these three are one.

So, again, the word, sovereign, does not appear in the Bible but the definition does. Before we get to the Bible verses, let us look at the definition of Sovereign in the dictionary. The dictionary being used will be the "The American Dictionary of the English Language" by Noah Webster in 1828. The definitions are as follows:

Sovereign: noun: a supreme lord or ruler; one who possesses the highest authority.

Sovereignty: noun: Supreme power; supremacy; the possession of the highest power.

With this being said, the only one that has supreme power and authority is God alone.

Now, lets get into the Bible verses that use the definition of the word, sovereign.

The first thing that we will get to is the verses in the Bible that use the word, "Almighty." This word appears 57 times in the Old and New Testaments. In the Old Testament there is only one Hebrew word for "Almighty." The Strongs # is H7706. It appears 48 times. Every time it is the English word, "Almighty." The Hebrew word is "Shadday." In the New Testament there is only one Greek word for "Almighty" and the Strong's # is G3841. It appears 10 times. It is translated 9 times "Almighty" and one time, "Omnipotent."

The Versus from the Old Testament using the word, "Almighty" (48 Times)

(Gen 17:1) And when Abram was ninety years old and nine, the LORD appeared to Abram, and said unto him, **I *am* the Almighty God**; walk before me, and be thou perfect.

(Gen 28:3) And **God Almighty** bless thee, and make thee fruitful, and multiply thee, that thou mayest be a multitude of people;

(Gen 35:11) And God said unto him, **I *am* God Almighty**: be fruitful and multiply; a nation and a company of nations shall be of thee, and kings shall come out of thy loins;

(Gen 43:14) And <u>**God Almighty**</u> give you mercy before the man, that he may send away your other brother, and Benjamin. If I be bereaved *of my children*, I am bereaved.

(Gen 48:3) And Jacob said unto Joseph<u>**, God Almighty**</u> appeared unto me at Luz in the land of Canaan, and blessed me,

(Gen 49:25) *Even* by the God of thy father, who shall help thee; and by <u>**the Almighty**</u>, who shall bless thee with blessings of heaven above, blessings of the deep that lieth under, blessings of the breasts, and of the womb:

(Exod 6:3) And I appeared unto Abraham, unto Isaac, and unto Jacob, by *the name of* <u>**God Almighty**</u>, but by my name JEHOVAH was I not known to them.

(Num 24:4) He hath said, which heard the words of God, which saw the vision of <u>**the Almighty**</u>, falling *into a trance*, but having his eyes open:

(Num 24:16) He hath said, which heard the words of God, and knew the knowledge of the most High, *which* saw the vision of <u>**the Almighty**</u>, falling *into a trance*, but having his eyes open:

(Ruth 1:20) And she said unto them, Call me not Naomi, call me Mara: for <u>**the Almighty**</u> hath dealt very bitterly with me.

(Ruth 1:21) I went out full, and the LORD hath brought me home again empty: why *then* call ye me Naomi, seeing the LORD hath testified against me, and **the Almighty** hath afflicted me?

(Job 5:17) Behold, happy *is* the man whom God correcteth: therefore despise not thou the chastening of **the Almighty**:

(Job 6:4) For the arrows of **the Almighty** *are* within me, the poison whereof drinketh up my spirit: the terrors of God do set themselves in array against me.

(Job 6:14) To him that is afflicted pity *should be shewed* from his friend; but he forsaketh the fear of **the Almighty**.

(Job 8:3) Doth God pervert judgment? or doth **the Almighty** pervert justice?

(Job 8:5) If thou wouldest seek unto God betimes, and make thy supplication to **the Almighty**;

(Job 11:7) Canst thou by searching find out God? canst thou find out **the Almighty** unto perfection?

(Job 13:3) Surely I would speak to **the Almighty**, and I desire to reason with God.

(Job 15:25) For he stretcheth out his hand against God, and strengtheneth himself against **the Almighty.**

(Job 21:15) What *is* **the Almighty**, that we should serve him? and what profit should we have, if we pray unto him?

(Job 21:20) His eyes shall see his destruction, and he shall drink of the wrath of **the Almighty**.

(Job 22:3) *Is it* any pleasure to **the Almighty**, that thou art righteous? or *is it* gain *to him*, that thou makest thy ways perfect?

(Job 22:17) Which said unto God, Depart from us: and what can **the Almighty** do for them?

(Job 22:23) If thou return to **the Almighty**, thou shalt be built up, thou shalt put away iniquity far from thy tabernacles.

(Job 22:25) Yea, **the Almighty** shall be thy defence, and thou shalt have plenty of silver.

(Job 22:26) For then shalt thou have thy delight in **the Almighty**, and shalt lift up thy face unto God.

(Job 23:16) For God maketh my heart soft, and **the Almighty** troubleth me:

(Job 24:1) Why, seeing times are not hidden from **the Almighty**, do they that know him not see his days?

(Job 27:2) *As* God liveth, *who* hath taken away my judgment; and **the Almighty**, *who* hath vexed my soul;

(Job 27:10) Will he delight himself in **the Almighty**? will he always call upon God?

(Job 27:11) I will teach you by the hand of God: *that* which *is* with **the Almighty** will I not conceal.

(Job 27:13) This *is* the portion of a wicked man with God, and the heritage of oppressors, *which* they shall receive of **the Almighty.**

(Job 29:5) When **the Almighty** *was* yet with me, *when* my children *were* about me;

(Job 31:2) For what portion of God *is there* from above? and *what* inheritance of **the Almighty** from on high?

(Job 31:35) Oh that one would hear me! behold, my desire *is, that* **the Almighty** would answer me, and *that* mine adversary had written a book.

(Job 32:8) But *there is* a spirit in man: and the inspiration of **the Almighty** giveth them understanding.

(Job 33:4) The Spirit of God hath made me, and the breath of **the Almighty** hath given me life.

(Job 34:10) Therefore hearken unto me, ye men of understanding: far be it from God, *that he should do* wickedness; and *from* **the Almighty**, *that he should commit* iniquity.

(Job 34:12) Yea, surely God will not do wickedly, neither will **the Almighty** pervert judgment.
(Job 35:13) Surely God will not hear vanity, neither will **the Almighty** regard it.

(Job 37:23) *Touching* **the Almighty**, we cannot find him out: *he is* excellent in power, and in judgment, and in plenty of justice: he will not afflict.

(Job 40:2) Shall he that contendeth with **the Almighty** instruct *him*? he that reproveth God, let him answer it.

(Ps 68:14) When **the Almighty** scattered kings in it, it was *white* as snow in Salmon.

(Ps 91:1) He that dwelleth in the secret place of the most High shall abide under the shadow of **the Almighty**.

(Isa 13:6) Howl ye; for the day of the LORD *is* at hand; it shall come as a destruction from **the Almighty.**

(Ezek 1:24) And when they went, I heard the noise of their wings, like the noise of great waters, as the voice of **the Almighty**, the voice of speech, as the noise of an host: when they stood, they let down their wings.

(Ezek 10:5) And the sound of the cherubims' wings was heard *even* to the outer court, as the voice of **the Almighty God** when he speaketh.

(Joel 1:15) Alas for the day! for the day of the LORD *is* at hand, and as a destruction from the **Almighty** shall it come.

The Verses from the New Testament using the word, "Almighty" (10 Times)

(2Cor 6:18) And will be a Father unto you, and ye shall be my sons and daughters, saith the **Lord Almighty**.

(Rev 1:8) I am Alpha and Omega, the beginning and the ending, saith the Lord, which is, and which was, and which is to come, **the Almighty**.

(Rev 4:8) And the four beasts had each of them six wings about *him*; and *they were* full of eyes within: and they rest not day and night, saying, Holy, holy, holy, **Lord God Almighty**, which was, and is, and is to come.

(Rev 11:17) Saying, We give thee thanks, O **Lord God Almighty**, which art, and wast, and art to come;

because thou hast taken to thee thy great power, and hast reigned.

(Rev 15:3) And they sing the song of Moses the servant of God, and the song of the Lamb, saying, Great and marvellous *are* thy works, **Lord God Almighty**; just and true *are* thy ways, thou King of saints.

(Rev 16:7) And I heard another out of the altar say, Even so, **Lord God Almighty**, true and righteous *are* thy judgments.

(Rev 16:14) For they are the spirits of devils, working miracles, *which* go forth unto the kings of the earth and of the whole world, to gather them to the battle of that great day of **God Almighty**.

(Rev 19:6) And I heard as it were the voice of a great multitude, and as the voice of many waters, and as the voice of mighty thunderings, saying, Alleluia: for the **Lord God omnipotent** reigneth.

(Rev 19:15) And out of his mouth goeth a sharp sword, that with it he should smite the nations: and he shall rule them with a rod of iron: and he treadeth the winepress of the fierceness and wrath of **Almighty God**.

(Rev 21:22) And I saw no temple therein: for **the Lord God Almighty** and the Lamb are the temple of it.

As you can see from the above verses, the word, "Almighty," is always used with God and always refers to God.

God is King of Kings and Lord of Lords

1Tim 6:13 I give thee charge in the sight of God, who quickeneth all things, and *before* Christ Jesus, who before Pontius Pilate witnessed a good confession;

1Tim 6:14 That thou keep *this* commandment without spot, unrebukeable, until the appearing of our Lord Jesus Christ:

1Tim 6:15 Which in his times **he shall shew, *who is* the blessed and only Potentate, the King of kings, and Lord of lords;**

1Tim 6:16 Who only hath immortality, dwelling in the light which no man can approach unto; whom no man hath seen, nor can see: to whom *be* honour and power everlasting. Amen.

(Rev 17:14) These shall make war with the Lamb, and **the Lamb shall overcome them: for he is Lord of lords, and King of kings**: and they that are with him *are* called, and chosen, and faithful.

Rev 19:11 And I saw heaven opened, and behold a white horse; and he that sat upon him *was* called Faithful and True, and in righteousness he doth judge and make war.

Rev 19:12 His eyes *were* as a flame of fire, and on his head *were* many crowns; and he had a name written, that no man knew, but he himself.

Rev 19:13 And he *was* clothed with a vesture dipped in blood: and **his name is called The Word of God.**

Rev 19:14 And the armies *which were* in heaven followed him upon white horses, clothed in fine linen, white and clean.

Rev 19:15 And out of his mouth goeth a sharp sword, that with it he should smite the nations: and he shall rule them with a rod of iron: and he treadeth the winepress of the fierceness and wrath of **Almighty God.**

Rev 19:16 And he hath on *his* vesture and on his thigh a name written, **KING OF KINGS, AND LORD OF LORDS.**

So, from the above verses on "Almighty" and "King of kings" and "Lord of lords", these verses tell us that God alone is **"Sovereign."**

It seems to be taught by Calvinists that the doctrines on Adoption, Predestination, Election, and Foreknowledge are all teachings of Sovereignty and shoots over the heads of your average believer.

Allow me to clarify. The Bible is given by a sovereign God and written by a sovereign God and persevered by a sovereign God. Every teaching in the Bible and every doctrine in the Bible is given by a sovereign God. To elevate these teachings on Adoption, Predestination, Election, and Foreknowledge as superior and present the impression that only a Calvinist can understand these teachings is totally arrogant and false.

There are teachings in the Bible that are classified as Cardinal Doctrines and must be believed in order to be saved. Please see this author's book on "Cardinal Doctrines." Allow me to give you a partial list of these Cardinal doctrines. They are as follows:

1. The Bible is the Word of God
2. Jesus is the Son of God
3. Jesus is God the Son
4. Jesus is the Christ
5. The Virgin Birth of Christ
6. The Blood Atonement
7. All mankind are Sinners in need of Salvation
8. Jesus came in human Flesh
9. The Gospel is the death, burial, and resurrection of Christ
10. The Trinity; God the Father; God the Son; and God the Holy Spirit
11. Jesus is the only way into heaven.

For the Calvinist to suggest that the teaching on Adoption, Predestination, Election, and Foreknowledge are superior to the point that the non-Calvinist cannot comprehend them is simply not true. Notice the point in the following passage.

Deut 29:29 <u>The secret *things belong* unto the LORD our God: but those *things which are* revealed *belong* unto us and to our children for ever</u>, that *we* may do all the words of this law.

The Bible has been revealed to us by the Sovereign God and every teaching in the Bible belongs to everyone of God's people.

2Tim 3:16 All scripture *is* given by inspiration of God, and *is* profitable for doctrine, for reproof, for correction, for instruction in righteousness: **2Tim 3:17** That the man of God may be perfect, throughly furnished unto all good works.

2Pet 1:20 Knowing this first, that no prophecy of the scripture is of any private interpretation. **2Pet 1:21** For the prophecy came not in old time by the will of man: but holy men of God spake *as they were* moved by the Holy Ghost.

So, we as believers have a Holy Book written by a Sovereign God who tells us that all have sinned and that we are incapable of paying for our own sins and that whosoever wants to be saved can be saved and that Jesus died for the entire human race and after trusting Christ as our Savior, we are eternally secure because God hangs on to us and not because we are trying to hang on to God.

Printed in the United States
By Bookmasters